A STILL MOMENT

Essays on the Art of

Eudora Welty

edited by

JOHN F. DESMOND

The Scarecrow Press, Inc.
Metuchen, N.J. & London
1978

Library of Congress Cataloging in Publication Data

Main entry under title:

A still moment.

    Includes index.
    CONTENTS: Introduction.--Harris, J. The real
thing.--Allen, J. A. Eudora Welty.--Neault, D. J.
Time in the fiction of Eudora Welty. [etc.]
    1. Welty, Eudora, 1909-   --Criticism and
interpretation--Addresses, essays, lectures.
I. Desmond, John F.
PS3545.E6Z87   813'.5'2   78-3719
ISBN 0-8108-1129-4

ACKNOWLEDGMENTS

For permission to use material reprinted in this book, the editor is grateful to the following publishers and copyright holders:

Random House, Inc.   For permission to quote from Losing Battles and The Optimist's Daughter, by Eudora Welty.   Copyright © 1970 and 1969, 1972 respectively.

Harcourt Brace Jovanovich, Inc.   For permission to quote from the following works by Eudora Welty: Delta Wedding, copyright © 1945, 1946.   The Wide Net and Other Stories, copyright © 1943.   A Curtain of Green, copyright © 1936, 1937, 1938, 1939, 1941.   The Ponder Heart, copyright © 1953, 1954.   The Bride of the Innisfallen, copyright © 1949, 1951, 1952, 1954, 1955.   The Robber Bridegroom, copyright © 1942.   The Golden Apples, copyright © 1947, 1948, 1949.   Short Stories, copyright © 1949.

Russell and Volkening, Inc.   For permission to quote from the following works by Eudora Welty: Three Papers on Fiction, copyright © 1962.   "Place in Fiction," copyright © 1956.

The Virginia Quarterly Review.   For permission to reprint John A. Allen's "Eudora Welty: The Three Moments" from The Virginia Quarterly Review, vol. 51 (Autumn 1975), 605-627.

RANAM.   For permission to reprint M. E. Bradford's "Looking Down from a High Place: the Serenity of Miss Welty's Losing Battles" from RANAM, vol. IV (1971), 92-97.

The editor also wishes to acknowledge gratefully the assistance of Professor William McMillen, whose inspiration and editorial aid have helped make this collection possible, and to acknowledge Whitman College, Walla Walla, Washington, for their support of this project.

TABLE OF CONTENTS

v

INTRODUCTION

Referring to the English novelist Henry Green, Eudora Welty once said: "The heart may quail, but the mind applauds: if there must be any analyses about this writer (and this certainly is in the air) let there be many, all different." The remark might equally as well be applied to Miss Welty's fiction, for after a period of relative dormancy, analyses of her work are once again "in the air," spurred especially by the publication of Losing Battles and The Optimist's Daughter. It is improbable that the analyses will be "all different" (one detects both the wisdom and whimsy in her remark about Green), but if so it will likely be due less to the critical eclecticism of our age than to the protean and myriad forms her imagination has taken during her forty years or so of fiction writing.

It has become a commonplace among scholars to acknowledge that Miss Welty has never received the wide audience her talent as a writer so richly deserves. One reason frequently offered is because of her supposed preciosity of style; the argument runs that her sensitivity and power of language outstrip the matter of her stories. Another reason given is that she has deliberately chosen not to follow the fictional mainstream of her day--social realism built on an existentialist foundation. Some critics have admired and applauded her skill in using myth in her work, as one might admire the intricate design of a piece of Dresden china. Yet even here, as deep as the admiration may go, there is an underlying sentiment that somehow her work does not speak to our modern predicament directly enough, and that her achievements as an artist are not compensated by sufficient breadth of appeal. At this point one might begin to wonder if such a judgment does not in fact reveal our limitations as critics and readers, rather than a limitation in Miss Welty's work. I believe it does, and yet I also believe that this condition leads us directly into Welty's strength as a writer--to the good of her fiction, and to the reason her work will still be read when the current tides of critical and popular taste have turned and turned again.

Eudora Welty's fiction has not been as well appreciated as it should be because it is based upon a metaphysical sense of human existence, and in the main, as Eliot perceived long ago, our age has lost the sense of the metaphysical dimensions of reality. With the metaphysical sense has also gone the sense of mystery, the belief that, for better or worse, our lives are impenetrable in their essence. It is small wonder, therefore, that an apparent "gap" exists between Welty's vision and much of the general thought of our day. Yet beneath the many shapes her fictional world has given us lies a constant and unchanging core, a metaphysical sense which informs every mode of being she examines: personality, time, eternity, memory, dream, love, beauty, aloneness--all of those motions of the spirit which are incapable of exhaustion. This is her continuing gift to readers who will accept it, and if fiction is able to teach us how to live, as we know it can, then there is no better guide to the heart's abiding truths than Miss Welty's fiction. The essays in this collection are intended as aids to understanding the Weltian vision, so that we might not only be better able to give the author her due, but also through her to be recalled to our essential selves.

John F. Desmond,
Whitman College,
Walla Walla,
Washington

THE REAL THING:
Eudora Welty's Essential Vision

by Jerry Harris

> Certainly a story and its analysis are not the mir-
> ror opposites of each other.... The main differ-
> ence is in world-surround. One surround is a
> vision and the other is a pattern for good visions
> (which--who knows!--fashion may have tweaked a
> little) or the nicest, carefullest black-and-white
> tracing that a breath of life would do for. Each,
> either, or neither may be a masterpiece of con-
> struction; but the products are not to be confused.
>
> --Eudora Welty in "How I Write"[1]

Ruth M. Vande Kieft, author of the first and best of
the full-length studies of Eudora Welty's works, says that
Miss Welty's "stories tell us something about her philosophical vision, which might be identified (at the risk of giving
her work the 'tweak of fashion' she deplores) as pessimistic
and existential."[2] I believe that Vande Kieft has indeed suc-
cumbed to the risk she notes, but it is not difficult to see
how she could do so even with good intentions to avoid it.
The distinction between existentialism and Miss Welty's philosophical vision as it is revealed in her writings seems a
fine one at first, but I think a careful tracing of the line of
her thought reveals that distinction to be definite and, in addition, important to an understanding of her art.

Any discussion of Eudora Welty's fiction in terms of
philosophical categories should, of course, note that Miss
Welty has strong feelings about the relationship between
philosophy and fiction:

1

> I don't think any ideas come to you from other peo-
> ple's minds, when you're writing, as directives.
> You can't take hints and suggestions from this per-
> son and that to know where you're going. It's just
> outside the whole process of writing a story.   That
> all has to come from within.   It doesn't mean that
> you haven't read things and understood things through
> reading and come to think things through reading
> that don't filter down and apply.... [But] When
> you're writing, your influences are by way of the
> imagination only.... I think of my source as real
> life itself--nothing to do with reference books. 3

Miss Welty, then, is more concerned with the relationship between fiction and reality than with the relationship
between fiction and schools of philosophic thought. In fact,
the writing of her much admired fiction apparently began con-
currently with a heightened concern about the relationship between fiction and reality.   According to her own testimony,
she changed from a writer of juvenilia into a mature writer
when she began to "get some sonoc" and "see the great rift
between what I wrote and what was the real thing."4   The
juvenile stories were set in Paris, and one of them began:
"Monsieur Boule deposited a delicate dagger in Mademoiselle's
left side and departed with poised immediacy." "Poised immediacy" pleased her greatly, but she was writing, she says,
about something of which she was "totally ignorant."   Creation of the Eudora Welty stories we read began when "I went
home and started writing about what I know."

Therefore, even though Miss Welty is more concerned
with how her stories match up against life than against "reference books," her attitude toward fiction is very much involved in a philosophic issue; the relationship between fiction
and reality is a problem in aesthetics, epistomology, and ultimately metaphysics.   Furthermore, in her nonfiction Miss
Welty has made explicit statements about this problem that
can quite legitimately be used to relate her to categories of
philosophic thought.

Here is an example, both particularly excellent and
generally typical, of her attempts to "express outside fiction"
what she thinks "the heart of fiction" is:

> As a child I was led, an unwilling sightseer,
> into Mammoth Cave in Kentucky, and after our
> party had been halted in the blackest hole yet and

our guide had let us wait guessing in cold dark
what would happen to us, suddenly a light was
struck. And we stood in a prism. The chamber
was bathed in color and there was nothing else,
we and our guide were blotted out by radiance.
As I remember, nobody said Boo. Gradually we
could make out that there was a river in the floor,
black as night, that appeared to come out of a closet in the wall; and then on it a common rowboat,
with ordinary countrified people like ourselves sitting in it, mute, wearing hats, came floating out
and on by and exited into the closet in the opposite
wall. I suppose they were simply a party taking
the more expensive tour. As we tourists mutually
and silently stared, our guide treated us to a recitation on bats, how they lived in uncounted numbers
down here and reached light by shooting up winding
mile-high chimneys through rock, never touching by
so much as the crook of a wing. He had memorized
the speech, and we didn't see a bat. Then the light
was put out--just as after you've had your two cents'
worth in the Baptistry of Florence, where of course
more happens: the thing I'm trying here to leave
out. As again we stood damp and cold and not able
to see our feet, while we each now had something
of our own out of it, presumably, and liking it or
not, what I for one remember is how right I had
been in telling my parents it would be a bore. For
I was too ignorant to know there might be more,
or even less, in there than I could see unaided.

Fiction is not the cave; and human life, fiction's territory, merely contains caves. I am only
trying to express what I think the so-called raw
material is without its interpretation; without its
artist. Without the act of human understanding,
and it is a double act through which we make sense
to each other, experience is the worst kind of emptiness, it is obliteration, black or prismatic, as
meaningless as was indeed that loveless cave. Before there is meaning, there has to occur some personal act of vision; and it is this that is continu-
ously projected as the novelist writes and again as
we, each to ourselves, read.

If this makes fiction sound full of mystery,
I think it's fuller than I know how to say.... The
mystery lies in the use of language to express human life.[5]

Because Miss Welty here depicts human existence as threatened by mammoth caverns of meaningless and as granted the salvation of meaning only by "some personal act of vision," she seems very much in tune with contemporary thinking. We live in the age of Heisenberg's indeterminacy, Sartre's existentialism, Camus' absurdity, Stevens's aestheticism, Robbe-Grillet's new novel, and even--an article in a recent number of Modern Fiction Studies declares--a "new solipsism."6 Many of us feel that the only real thing we can unblushingly acknowledge is the experience of confrontation between frustrated subjectivity and unyielding chaos. Eudora Welty lives in this age also and, perceptive lady that she is, fully participates in the concerns which produce this sense of what is real, participates so fully that she often sounds like a member of the faith. To a significant extent, however, she is a heretic.

As an illustration of this situation, Miss Welty's ideas can be contrasted with those expressed in Frank Kermode's book The Sense of an Ending: Studies in the Theory of Fiction. Kermode's theory, I assume, can reasonably be called existentialist: "Men, like poets, rush 'into the middest,' in medias res, when they are born; they also die in mediis rebus, and to make sense of their span they need fictive concords with origins and ends, such as give meaning to lives and to poems."7 There are passages in Eudora Welty's writings about the theory of fiction which could be inserted into one of Kermode's less latinate pages without creating much notice of a change in authors: "The novel or story ended, shape must have made its own impression on the reader, so that he feels that some design in life (by which I mean aesthetic pattern, not purpose) has just been discovered there."8

As I have said, it is easy to see how Ruth Vande Kieft could label Miss Welty an existentialist without feeling she was succumbing to the tweak of fashion. But there is a significant difference between Eudora Welty's attitudes and those of Kermode. Initially it may seem a very fine distinction, a matter of difference only in emphasis. For Kermode "fictive concords" are something we need to save us from the madness of being simply in "the middest" without a sense of beginning or end. To keep that need satisfied as long as possible, to keep the satisfaction as safe as possible (ultimately it will be impossible to keep it safe), Kermode wants fictions that exercise "clerical scepticism": "... fictions too easy we call 'escapist'; we want them not only to console but to make discoveries of hard truth here and now, in

the middest. "[9] What he seems to be saying is that we want
good escapist fictions, not bad; fictions that have enough of
"hard truth here and now" to make the consolation, the escape, believable.   Here is Miss Welty's way of treating virtually the same subject: ". . . it is not to escape his life
but more to pin it down (though by pinning it down he no
doubt does escape it a little) that a writer writes. . . . "[10]
Thus if we equate "hard truth" and "pinning it down" on one
hand and "escape" and "consolation" on the other, it appears
that Kermode and Miss Welty see both as encompassed within the accomplishment of good fiction, but that Kermode's
emphasis is on the importance of "escape" while Miss Welty's
is on the importance of "hard truth. "

However, it is likely that Kermode would respond to
Miss Welty's statement by saying that to pin life down is not
just to escape "a little" but is precisely consolation and escape.   From this it is clear that we are dealing not with
merely a difference in emphasis but with a difference about
the nature of human existence and of fiction.   For Kermode,
reality is subjectivity and external chaos forever separated,
and ultimately all "concord" between them is nothing but con-
soling fiction.   For Miss Welty the case is different, as is
best expressed in another of her images intended to state
"outside of fiction" what she thinks is "the heart of fiction":

> Some of us grew up with the china night-light, the
> little lamp whose lighting showed its secret and
> with that spread enchantment.   The outside is
> painted with a scene, which is one thing; then,
> when the lamp is lighted, through the porcelain
> sides a new picture comes out through the old,
> and they are seen as one.   A lamp I knew of was
> a view of London till it was lit; but then it was
> the Great Fire of London, and you could go beau-
> tifully to sleep by it.   The lamp alight is the com-
> bination of internal and external, these inner and
> outer surfaces do lie so close together and so im-
> plicit in each other, the wonder is that human life
> so often separates them, or appears to, and it
> takes a good novel to put them back together. [11]

For Miss Welty reality is not frustrated subjectivity
confronting unyielding chaos.   The chaos is only real as
"raw material. "   "Fiction is not the cave; and human life,
fiction's territory, merely contains caves. "   Reality is "the
combination of internal and external" as revealed by the glow

of intuitive imagination, and any vision of internal and external as irreconcilably separate can only be "a wonder,"
a wonder of wrongheadedness.

Eudora Welty can be partially characterized by the
terms she has used to characterize Henry Green. [12] She
calls him a "romantic artist ... whose senses and whose
temperament are and have remained romantic and whose
reason and experience are lying in wait for the romantic at
every turn."[13] By having reason and experience "lying in
wait for the romantic," she exercises what Kermode would
call "clerical scepticism," but that is not enough to keep
internal and external separate, as they are for Kermode.
This can be seen in her response to another mode of writing about contemporary fiction--a mode from which she is
more obviously different than from Kermode's: "Surely what
is indicated is not to confess ourselves, but to commit ourselves. Only when the best writer on earth is ready and
willing, and of course able, to commit himself to his subject can he truly know it--that is, absorb it, embrace it in
his mind, take it to his heart, speak it in plain words."[14]
This is not the Sartrean commitment, but the commitment
that makes possible romantic intuition of ultimate truth:
"For the spirit of things is what is sought."[15]

Miss Welty's "experience and reason lie in wait for
the romantic" to an extent that gives her enough "clerical
scepticism" to know that we cannot expect different intuitions
to arrive at identical truths: "There must surely be as
many ways of seeing a place as there are pairs of eyes to
see it. The impact happens in different ways." Nevertheless, unlike Kermode, she has not utterly abandoned the
hope that the "as" of fiction can become the "is" of reality:[16]
"It may be the stranger within the gates whose eye is smitten
by the crucial thing, the essence of life, the moment or act
in our long-familiar midst that will forever define it."[17]

According to Kermode, the "as" of fiction cannot
become the "is" of reality because reality is the chaos of
always being in "the middest," while fiction cannot escape
form, cannot escape some sense of beginning, middle, and
end: "Even when there is a profession of complete anarchy,
as in ... a poem such as Patterson, which rejects as spuri-
ous whatever most of us regard as form, it seems that time
will always reveal some congruence with a paradigm--provided
always that there is in the work that necessary element of
the customary which enables it to communicate at all."[18]

Therefore, Kermode sees imitative form as indeed a fallacy.
He prefers, for example, Sartre's fiction to Robbe Grillet's:
"Sartre knew ... that his book [Nausea], though it surrounds
the hero with images of formlessness, inhumanity, nausea,
must not itself be formless or viscous or inhuman, any more
than it may repeat the formal presumptuousness of the nine-
teenth-century novel or the arrogant omniscience of Mauriac.
It works somewhere between these extremes...."[19] Nausea
pleases Kermode because it has enough form--"some congruence with a paradigm"--to communicate and because what
it communicates concerns the perpetual attempts of subjectivity to impose order on a perpetually resistant and always
ultimately victorious external chaos.   Kermode's theory of
fiction must see Nausea as "something of a model"[20] because
Kermode (and Sartre) see reality as separation of the internal
and the external.

Because Eudora Welty sees reality as "the combination
of the internal and the external," because she seeks in that
combination "the spirit of things," "the essence of life," she
can legitimately posit the theory that fiction, although it is
a lie, can nevertheless aim at achieving the magical and
mysterious accomplishment of being ordered and yet true.
While Kermode acknowledges the necessity of form, it is a
grudging acknowledgment which disparages form because it
is what prevents "as" from ever being "is."   Miss Welty,
on the other hand, can celebrate form while acknowledging,
without any grudge, that fiction shouldn't get too tidy.   She
thinks, in fact, that beauty in fiction comes from form.
Probably Kermode would agree, but if so, his philosophical
position makes it difficult to celebrate beauty.   Miss Welty's
puts her under no such constraints: "Beauty is of form, development of idea, or after effect ... [her ellipsis] it often
comes from carefulness, lack of confusion, elimination of
waste--and yes, those are the rules.   But that can on occasion be a cold kind of beauty, when there are warm kinds.
And beware of tidiness.   Sometimes spontaneity is the most
sparkling kind of beauty...."[21]

Also, because Eudora Welty sees reality as "the combination of the internal and the external" out of which can be
intuited "the spirit of things," "the essence of life," she does
not have the sense of crisis Kermode has about the difference
between the external chaos and the order in a work of fiction.
Rather than having a sense of crisis about it, she merely
speaks of

> ... the interesting disparity between integrity
> --which merges in a story as truth or validity--and
> plausibility.   The validity of everyday life is notor-
> iously dependent on certain things.   The validity of
> a story--not quite so notoriously--depends on things
> of an entirely different order.   There's no need to
> hedge about--the two validities conflict.   That is,
> there was never any question of their tallying.
>   I don't think myself it makes much differ-
> ence.   The term plausibility comes from the every-
> day world and if put to measure the story world,
> the plausibility falls down, not the story. [22]

"There is no need to hedge about" and there is no sense of
crisis either; "there was never any question" of the validity
of everyday life and the validity of fiction "tallying."   There
is no sense of crisis in this issue for Miss Welty because
she feels that, measured against artistic integrity, the mere
plausibility of the external world "falls down."   It is just
not as valid, not as true--wondrous and mysterious as that
seems.   A great mystery indeed is "the use of language to
express human life."

     Mystery and magic are two extremely important words
in Miss Welty's lexicon, and they are words that would be
strange on the pages of Kermode or Sartre, especially if they
were delivered in the tone Eudora Welty gives them.   The
mystery of fiction is that a good novel or short story can put
back together the internal and external worlds that "human
life so often separates" and by so doing capture "the spirit
of things," something more real than the chaos of the external surface.   Miss Welty says that Henry James in his
story "The Real Thing" presents "a good case for the validity of what is represented over what is real" (that is, real
in terms of the separate external world).   She points out
that the low-born characters, Miss Churm and the Italian,
are better models for the illustrator who narrates the story
than are Major and Mrs. Monarch because "it is Miss Churm's
and the Italian's nature to work out perfectly, representing
ladies and gentlemen, for they are receptive to ideas 'on the
wing,' yield and abandon themselves over to them at once,
and fit perfectly as the thing they represent."[23]   To create
the contrast between this ability and Mrs. Monarch's real-
ness, Miss Welty quotes James: "Mrs. Monarch was always
a lady, certainly, and into the bargain was always the same
lady.   She was the real thing, but always the same thing."

Eudora Welty believes good fiction accomplishes the same magic Miss Churm and the Italian do. Fiction must be "receptive to ideas 'on the wing,' yield and abandon itself over to them at once," and to do that it cannot deal with each individual "real thing" in the external world. Instead, it must "accurately choose, combine, superimpose upon, blot out, shake up, alter the outside world.... "[24] It must do this because "it is the business of writing, and the responsibility of the writer, to disentangle the significant--in character, incident, setting, mood, everything--from the random and meaningless and irrelevant that in real life surround and beset it. It is the matter of his selecting and, by all that implies, of changing, 'real' life as he goes.... "[25] Only by achieving in this way a union of the external and the internal, a union which can represent "the spirit of things," "the crucial thing, the essence of life, the moment or act in our long familiar midst that will forever define it"; only in this way can fiction fulfill its responsibility: "Making reality real is art's responsibility. "[26] Art, then, "is ... the voice of the individual, doing its best to speak, not comfort of any sort, indeed, but truth. "[27]

Therefore, even though hers is a mind of one involved in her time, if we are going to use philosophical categories to speak of Eudora Welty, we will do better to call her something like a "romantic essentialist" rather than an existentialist, at least when we are characterizing her thinking as it appears in her nonfiction.

Notes

[1]"How I Write" has appeared in Virginia Quarterly 31 (Spring 1955): 240-61, and in Understanding Fiction, Cleanth Brooks and Robert Penn Warren, eds., 2nd edition (New York, Appleton, Century, Crofts, 1959), pp. 545-53. This particular passage occurs on p. 549 of the Brooks and Warren book.

[2]Eudora Welty (New Haven: Twayne, 1962), p. 33.

[3]Charles T. Bunting, "'The Interior World': An Interview with Eudora Welty," The Southern Review 8 (October 1972), 729-30.

[4]All quotations in this paragraph are from "An Interview with Miss Eudora Welty," by Robert van Gelder, which

appeared in New York Times Book Review, 14 June 1942.

[5]From "Words into Fiction," one of Three Papers on Fiction by Eudora Welty, published in connection with her term as William Allan Neilson Professor at Smith College (Northampton, Massachusetts, 1962).   The other two papers in this collection are "Place in Fiction," which appeared earlier in South Atlantic Quarterly 55 (January 1956), 57-72, and "The Short Story," which has been published in at least two other forms--Short Stories (New York: Harcourt and Brace, 1949), the most complete version, and "The Reading and Writing of Short Stories," Atlantic 83 (February and March 1949), 54-58, 46-49.

[6]Arlen J. Hansen, "The Celebration of Solipsism: A New Trend in American Fiction," Modern Fiction Studies 19 (Spring 1973), 5-16.

[7]Frank Kermode, The Sense of an Ending: Studies in the Theory of Fiction (New York: Oxford University Press, 1967), p. 7.

[8]"Words into Fiction," p. 84.

[9]Kermode, p. 179.

[10]"Words into Fiction," p. 24.

[11]Actually, this image is also inside her fiction. Not only Miss Welty, but several of the characters in Delta Wedding grew up with the china night-light she describes.

[12]Miss Welty's admiration for Green is incomprehensible to some of her admirers.   Putting aside the issue of Green's merit, it is clear from her writings about him that she sees in him an artistic kinship.   There are several instances, some of which will be mentioned below, where she either uses terms to describe him that she has also used to describe herself or uses terms to describe him that she would obviously be pleased to see used to describe herself.

[13]"Henry Green: A Novelist of the Imagination," Texas Quarterly 4 (Autumn 1961), 251.

[14]"Place in Fiction," 69.

[15]"Place in Fiction," 64.

[16]Kermode, p. 79.

[17]"Place in Fiction," 70.

[18]Kermode, p. 129.

[19]Kermode, p. 146.

[20]Kermode, p. 145.

[21]Short Stories, p. 51.

[22]Short Stories, p. 48.

[23]Short Stories, p. 49, Miss Welty' emphasis.

[24]"Place in Fiction," 64.

[25]"Place in Fiction," 61.

[26]"Place in Fiction," 67.

[27]"Place in Fiction," 58.

EUDORA WELTY: THE THREE MOMENTS*

by John A. Allen

The characters in Eudora Welty's fiction are fortunate
indeed, for they are conceived in kindness, justice and compassion by the imagination that creates them. In Miss Welty's
work, the strong and the weak, the magnanimous and the
mean alike, in every circumstance retain their human dignity.
"I don't have an ounce of revenge in my body,"[1] Edna Earle
Ponder assures her auditor, and the words may aptly be applied to the author of The Ponder Heart. The reader, too,
enjoys Miss Welty's evenhanded bounty. On every page she
tacitly gives him credit for being adequately prepared to face
the shock of truth, sufficiently enamored of the real to relish
its unexpected faces, rational enough to know that reason
yields in the end to mystery. Her view of life is not idealized, nor is it tough in the sense of denying mortal existence
its proper and inalienable graces. We are safe, in reading
a Welty novel, from being dinned at, scolded, hoodwinked,
lectured, flattered or condescended to. Secure from malice,
anger or contempt, we enjoy a vision of the world depicted
with an objectivity which is enriched by warmth and charity.
If Eudora Welty has a bias, it springs from affection for the
human race.

Three of Miss Welty's novels--Delta Wedding, The
Ponder Heart, and The Optimist's Daughter--unfold through
the consciousness of female characters. And these women
are also fair-minded and humane. Of course, they present
a feminine point of view; but this, in Miss Welty's work, is
a matter of perspective which does not involve distortion.
For Eudora Welty, showing the action of a novel through a

*Reprinted by permission of the author and publisher from
The Virginia Quarterly Review 51:4 (Autumn 1975), 605-27.

woman's eyes is not an act of aggression but of illumination.

To be sure, Miss Welty delights her readers with
the heroic antics of certain male characters: Uncle Daniel,
Mike Fink, Jamie Lockhart, Jack Renfro, Curly Stovall,
Major Bullock. However, as we will try to show, the sug-
gestion here is not that male heroes are inherently ridiculous
but that these characters are not, at least initially, true
heroes at all. Criteria for genuine heroism as Miss Welty
sees it can be found obliquely conveyed throughout her fiction.
The work of demolition--to call it that--which she performs
upon the conventional image of the male hero has the effect
not of attacking the male sex and its image of itself but of
clearing the way for a conception of heroic action which does
fuller justice to the actual potentialities for heroism in men
and women alike.

II

In the sense suggested above, the tendency of Eudora
Welty's fiction is indeed anti-heroic; that is, it makes legit-
imate fun of the posturing male hero-adventurer whose main
objective, to paraphrase Uncle Curtis in Losing Battles, is
to butt the world like a billy goat and make it pay him heed. [2]
An appropriate emblem of this species of hero is the Perseus
of Greek myth; appropriate, that is, when Perseus' heroics
are taken at face value: He averts his eyes, swings the
magic sword, and lo!, with upraised arm he displays his
trophy--the snaky severed head of the Medusa. Thereafter,
he can use the Medusa-power as his own, striking his pose
again and again with gory trophy held on high to turn his
enemies to stone.

A survey of Miss Welty's heroes shows at once that
their achievements in the public eye bear only a marginal
resemblance to those of conquering Perseus. George Fairchild, as Ellen Fairchild correctly observes, is not "a chal-
lenger, a proud defier,"[3] although his family does conspire
to place him in that false position. On the other hand, Jack
Renfro, loser of battles, egged on by his adoring family,
challenges and defies to such disastrous effect that his father,
surveying the damages, can only say in wonder, "You couldn't
bring something like that to pass just by trying."[4] The most
flamboyant vaunting hero is the legendary Mike Fink of The
Robber Bridegroom. He drinks and brawls superbly but finds

himself demoted from king of the river boats to carrier of the territorial mails. He has been put down with shocking ease by brainy Jamie Lockhart, a bandit who also takes his lumps before he settles down with charming Rosamond to fatherhood and domesticity.

The female hero is Miss Welty's fiction may not be recognized at all as such by the unwary reader. Rosamond regularly faints in critical moments. Ellen Fairchild, from the outside, is simply a preoccupied mother of eight. And when Laurel McKelva in The Optimist's Daughter raises a weapon over her adversary's head, she does not complete the blow but arrests it in mid-air. Even that most staunch and pertinacious of heroes, Miss Julia Mortimer of Losing Battles, proves no match for her particular dragon; and Miss Beulah Renfro says of her with some justice, "Taking over more'n her territory, that was her downfall."[5]

III

The interpretation of the Perseus myth in The Golden Apples is put forward by Miss Welty through the thoughts of that book's hero, Virgie Rainey. She appears in "June Recital" as by far the most talented piano pupil of Miss Lotte Elisabeth Eckhart; then we lose sight of her for twenty-five years before, on the occasion of her mother's death, she re-enters the story in "The Wanderers." On the morning after the funeral, Virgie has pulled up stakes and is about to leave Morgana for good. She is sitting on the stile in front of the courthouse in MacLain, enjoying the light rain and the solitude. Her thoughts turn back to Miss Eckhart and to a picture that had hung on one of her walls--Perseus with the head of Medusa. "The vaunting was what she remembered, that uplifted arm."[6] Yet it is not the image of the hero triumphant that has become a permanent part of her mind but the stroke of the sword he wielded. "Cutting off the Medusa's head," she thinks,

> was the heroic act, perhaps, that made visible a horror in life, that was at once the horror in love ...--the separateness.[7]

The stroke of Perseus is not, in itself, a triumph of any kind. So far from ridding the world of a horror, it reveals one. It is not an act of liberation, not even an assertion of the sovereign will. The important thing, for Virgie, is not

what Perseus has done to Medusa; it is what the deed, like
a stroke of fate, has done to him.

The hero Virgie has in mind is not Perseus alone,
but a composite being, Perseus-Medusa, seen as one. Identification of the hero with the victim is essential to this conception of the heroic act:

> Because Virgie saw things in their time, like hear-
> ing them--and perhaps because she must believe
> in the Medusa equally with Perseus--she saw the
> stroke of the sword in three moments, not one. [8]

Realizing long after the fact that Miss Eckhart has taught
her far more than how to play the piano, Virgie recalls the
teacher herself as both hero and victim. All of Miss Welty's
teachers, and above all Miss Julia Mortimer, play this double
role. Gloria Renfro remembers Miss Julia's saying, "If it's
going to be a case of Saint George and the Dragon, I might
as well battle it left, right, front, back, center and side-
ways. "[9] As Gloria points out, "She was Saint George ...
And Ignorance was the dragon. "[10] Unhappily, the dragon
weathers this contest better than Saint George. Virgie's
Miss Eckhart, isolated from the beginning in Morgana by
her foreign origin and ways, had also fought a losing battle
and had also died in misery. She had seemed to fail even
with Virgie, who had done no more with her talent than play
background music at the Morgana picture show, who thought
she hated Miss Eckhart and had refused to greet the mad
old lady when they met for the last time on the streets of
Morgana. Yet, as we now discover,

> Virgie had not, after all, hated [Miss Eckhart] ...
> for she had taken Miss Eckhart's hate, and then
> her love, extracted them, the thorn and then the
> overflow--had hung the picture [of Perseus] on the
> wall for herself. She had absorbed the hero and
> the victim and then, stoutly, could sit down to the
> piano with all Beethoven ahead of her. [11]

In the first moment of the heroic stoke, the hero wields the
sword; in the second moment, he becomes the victim of that
stroke. In the third moment, he achieves some measure of
gain in understanding which leads on to self-renewal. Having
"absorbed the hero and the victim," Virgie had been able to
accept Miss Eckhart's gift of Beethoven- not Miss Eckhart's
Beethoven, but her own.

As hero, Virgie has seen the horror in life and love, vicariously through Miss Eckhart and her mother's life and death. She herself has felt the separateness which can cripple and kill, and they have not destroyed her. On the evening of her mother's death, "alone, untouched now, she felt like dancing; knowing herself not really, in her essence, yet hurt; and thus happy."[12] Although, in the eyes of the world, Virgie Rainey has achieved nothing noteworthy, she is, in her context in The Golden Apples, a type of the true hero. Her heroism does not derive from what is usually thought of as heroic action but from her capacity to feel and, through feeling, to know. Like a virgin goddess, an Artemis, she is self-sufficient and inviolable. The harmonious accord which she has reached exists between herself and natural things--the Big Black River, the moon--and within herself, where the eternal pair of mother and daughter, woman and child, continues to exist in peaceful oneness. Mother and daughter are the complementary elements of a whole feminine personality, a whole self. This is beautifully suggested by Miss Welty in the waking vision which comes to Virgie late at night after her mother's funeral:

> She knew that now at the river, where she had been before on moonlit nights in autumn, drunken and sleepless, mist lay on the water and filled the trees, and from the eyes to the moon would be a cone, a long silent horn, of white light. It was a connection, visible as the hair is in air, between the self and the moon, to make the self feel the child, a daughter far, far back.[13]

Virgie's uniqueness, the child in herself as the source of her renewal, is sometimes lost for a while, but it will always be returned. The mother, mistress of the cycles of natural things in time, will include her always, wherever and for however long she may remain a wanderer.

IV

Delta Wedding provides us with the counterpart of Virgie Rainey, a type of the male hero. The subject of heroism is explored and developed in fugue-like fashion in almost every corner of the book, in relation to every major character and even some of the minor ones. The main focus, however, is upon George Fairchild and Ellen Fairchild, his sister-in-law. The two characters are closely interrelated because there is a bond of feeling between them and because we see George mainly through the eyes and thoughts of Ellen.

The emblematic heroic act which is recalled and re-counted again and again in Delta Wedding concerns George as hero. The essentials of the incident are these: A group of Fairchilds find themselves on a railway trestle when the train, the Yellow Dog, approaches them. All but two of the group quickly jump to safety from the trestle to the dry creek bed below. But Maureen, a child of nine who is men-tally afflicted, has caught her shoe on the track and George is still trying to free her as the train bears down. At the last possible moment, Mr. Doolittle, the train's engineer, brings the train to a stop; and, by this simple miracle of fact, potential tragedy becomes the subject of anecdote, a tale to be told as one more bizarre incident in the Fairchild family history.

Throughout Delta Wedding it is George Fairchild who serves to set off in the minds of the other characters reflec-tions upon the association of feeling with knowing, and of both of these with acute perception of the outside world. For example, the thoughts of Shelley, the eldest Fairchild daughter, turn at one point on her memory of a tiny incident at a picnic, when a butterfly crossed the gaze of her Uncle George:

> She had then known something he knew all along, it seemed then--that when you felt, touched, heard, looked at things in the world, and found their fra-grances, they themselves made a sort of house within you, which filled with life to hold them, filled with knowledge all by itself, and all else, the other ways to know, seemed calculation and tyranny. 14

It is because George possesses the faculty which Shelley describes, and because his very presence inspires in others the recognition and exercise of that faculty in themselves, that one can say he is, so to speak, a full-time hero of the sort which Miss Welty celebrates.

In the mind of Ellen Fairchild, toward the end of Delta Wedding, George's habitual intensity of feeling is brought together with his public heroic act on the railway trestle. At that moment the heroic act emerges clearly as

an occasion when a quality of life in an individual meets and
responds to a challenge from fate. Ellen notices the dispar-
ity between the way in which she is coming to perceive the
meaning of the trestle incident and the meaning of it for
others in the Fairchild family:

> ... the family would forever see the stopping of
> the Yellow Dog ... as a preposterous diversion of
> their walk ... , for with the fatal chance removed
> the serious went with it forever, and only the ro-
> mantic and absurd abided. They would have nothing
> of the heroic, or the tragic now, thought Ellen,
> as though now she yielded up a heart's treasure. [15]

Here we have a valuable clue to the heart's treasure of
Miss Welty's fiction itself: the combination, in a kind of
double vision, of surface events which are preposterous, romantic and absurd with the inner perception and effect of
those events, which emerges as the essence of what is tragic
and heroic in human life.

George, Ellen goes on to reflect, "saw death on its
way, if [the others] did not. "[16] Like the bird in the house
in both Delta Wedding and The Optimist's Daughter, like
Laura McRaven whose loss of her mother makes her, for
the Fairchilds, "Insistently a little messenger or reminder
of death, "[17] the Yellow Dog superimposes death on heedless
and self-regarding life and sets the stage for the moment of
heroism. Seeking in her mind the true nature of George's
heroism, Ellen finds that it springs from "a quality of his
heart's intensity and his mind's. "[18] George regarded some
things,

> just things, in the outside world--with a passion
> which held him so still that it resembled indiffer-
> ence ... But ... shock, physical danger ... roused
> something in him that was immense contemplation,
> motionless pity, indifference. [19]

The heroic moment for George, as for other Welty characters, combines vaunting--"I'm damned if I wasn't going to
stand on that track if I wanted to!"[20]--with acceptance of
danger, the threat of change and its necessity. Further,
it combines both of these things, paradoxically, with the
capacity for strength in love. "He was capable," Ellen
thought,

> --taking no more prerogative than a kind of grace
> ... --of meeting a fate whose dealing out to him
> he would not contest ... And ... the darker in-
> stinct of a woman was satisfied that he was capable
> of the same kind of love.... [21]

George carries within himself the reconciliation of life and
death, of indifference and passion, which is the essence of
the third moment of the heroic act and which sums in itself
Virgie Rainey's understanding of the stroke of Perseus.

The emphasis, in Miss Welty's conception of the hero,
upon feeling and knowing applies to male and female alike.
However, this kind of experience seems to come more easily
to women than to men. Unlike George Fairchild as Ellen
sees him, male heroes on the conventional Perseus model
are likely to be preoccupied, up to a point, with a reckless
reliance on physical force like that of Jack Renfro's unfor-
tunate father, Ralph, who cripples himself with dynamite
just before his marriage to Miss Beulah and, some twenty
years later, still looks to dynamite for the solution to hard
problems:

> "He'll shortly blow up something else. He
> won't learn, he's a man," said Miss Lexie.
> "Yes sir, your touch is pure destruction!"
> Miss Beulah told him. [22]

Because, for all their own liability to error, women know
manfoolishness when they see it; they are often, in Miss
Welty's work, the teachers of their unwilling lovers and
husbands. In that capacity they are unflaggingly persistent
in their efforts to save their consorts from untimely ends
brought on by their extravagant behavior:

> "The system you're trying won't work,"
> Gloria said. "I wouldn't need to bring you down
> to earth if I wasn't your wife" [23]
> "... it's up to your wife to pit her common
> sense against you, Jack...." [24]

To be sure, it is Gloria's love and not her common sense
that works for Jack in the long run, but it would be futile
to deny that Miss Welty's women have her men beaten easily
when it comes to keeping their feet planted firmly on the
ground.

Rosamond, the charming ingénue in The Robber Bridegroom, is called upon not only to bring Jamie Lockhart down to earth but also, having accomplished that, to find the man beneath the disguise of lawlessness he wears. Fortunately, Rosamond's love, like Gloria's, never falters while she suffers one adversity after another at her lover's hands. When she first meets him, Jamie is a typically opportunistic male hero, his worse self always "out for a devilment of some kind."25 By day he is a respectable merchant, but by night, having stained his face with berry juice, he becomes the notorious Bandit of the Woods. What is worse, like other male heroes where women are concerned, he combines a theoretical high romanticism with an efficient bent for sexual brigandry. As romanticist, "in his heart Jamie carried nothing less than a dream of true love--something of gossamer and roses...."26 For this reason, he had been collecting clothes and jewels "that would deck a queen," but "as for finding this dream on earth, that Jamie was saving until the last...."27 One result of Jamie's romantic attitude is that when he first comes upon Rosamond in fancy dress, he strips the poor girl naked and ravishes not the girl but her clothes. At next encounter, however, he is all brigand and makes off with the maiden herself--not to become his dream on earth, but to serve perforce as housekeeper and bedmate for his robbers' den.

Rosamond's heroic act, her stripping away of Jamie's disguise, together with the consequences of her boldness, unfolds before us by degrees in an amusingly exact sequence of three moments. The prelude to the first moment begins when Rosamond, hiding behind a barrel in the robbers' den, witnesses the rape and murder of an Indian girl, the victim of Jamie's alter ego, a homicidal maniac named Little Harp. Though she remains concealed while the deed is done, Rosamond had heard the robbers swear to Little Harp that the Indian girl was none other than herself, and she "was almost ready to believe that she stood out in the room under the robbers' eyes and was not hiding down behind the barrel."28 Rosamond's curious intuition is, in fact, essentially correct. What she sees enacted before her eyes is her own plight as captive of the bandit king. Being ravished by an attractive stranger, however delightful it may be at first, is not without its penalty. Ignorance of her lover's name, as Rosamond begins to find, deprives her of her own, and such a loss is rape of individuality, a threat of murder to her own identity. As she puts it subsequently,

"My husband was a robber and not a bridegroom. . . .
He brought me his love under a mask, and kept
all the truth hidden from me . . . , and what I would
have given him he liked better to steal. "[29]

Now, in order to satisfy her longing for the secret truth,
she takes her courage in both hands and wipes the berry
stains from Jamie's face while he is sleeping.

The consequences of doing the necessary and forbidden
act, as always, are immediately disastrous. She recognizes
the King of the Bandits as Jamie Lockhart; and at the same
instant he recognizes her, alas, as "Clement Musgrove's
silly daughter. "[30] Charging angrily that Rosamond did not
trust him but only wanted to know who he was, Jamie dis-
appears through the window, and Rosamond, intent on following him, falls in the dust. Then, just before losing consciousness, "she felt the stirring within her that sent her a
fresh piece of news. "[31] The primary event of this first moment of the heroic act is, of course, Rosamond's successful
bravery or foolishness in finding the reality hidden behind
her lover's disguise. To find him is, of course, to lose
him, for she can never be the bandit's property again. But
a hint of the fruit of her continuing love, to arrive in due
course, simultaneously appears.

Not long after Rosamond regains consciousness, she
is presented with her second moment--another grizzly tab-
leau. This time the vision consists of a severed male head,
held up in Perseus fashion "at arm's length so it turned
round like a bird cage on a string. . . . "[32] This, it is clear,
is Jamie Lockhart's head by another name. It has a price
on it, and it will soon be displayed over Jamie's name on
a post in Rodney Square. Gazing upon it, Rosamond can
hardly fail to be aware of the horror which she has made
visible in her life and love. It is more than she is prepared
to cope with at that moment, and she swoons again. This
marks the end of the second moment, one in which Rosamond
identifies herself with the victim of her own heroic act. Of
course, if Rosamond only knew it, her disolation would be
eased by the fact that as there are two Jamies there are
also two heads; and one of them, that of the respectable merchant, is still fixed securely to the neck of its owner. But
Rosamond is unaware of this, and her sense of irredeemable
loss is unassuaged.

The third and final moment begins when Rosamond,

having recently awakened from her second swoon, is captured
by the Indians. These are a people who, being themselves
marked for early extinction, bear an aura of death about
them. Their camp in the Devil's Punch Bowl is a Land of
Shadows. Finding herself the prisoner of these savages,
Rosamond not unexpectedly swoons once more, and she is
borne away to the Indian camp to be sacrificed in revenge
for the slaughtered Indian maiden. The Land of the Dead
cannot, however, retain Rosamond long, any more than it
could retain her prototypes Persephone and Psyche, for these
women carry the secret of freedom within themselves. That
secret, of course, is faithful love. Through love's agency,
Rosamond's escape is soon accomplished, and Salome, the
wicked stepmother, is executed in her place. This is appropriate, for, unlike Rosamond, Salome loves no one whatso-
ever. She believes that she is subject to no power and is
by herself in the world: a philosophy dangerous at best and,
in this instance, fatal. Assured that Jamie is still alive,
and full of hope and confidence, Rosamond sets off to find
him and claim him for her own. The third moment has
brought renewal of life through a love that knows its object
truly. If anything has died, it is Rosamond's passion for
the Bandit of the Woods. The death of that outmoded sentiment clears the way not only for reunion of the lovers but
for the clear-eyed recognition by each of the other's true
identity, shorn of disguise.

VI

    In fairness to Jamie Lockhart it should be said that
his guide in casting off his role as Bandit of the Woods was
not the love of Rosamond alone. His reform was dramati-
cally accelerated by seeing his seamy side personified as
Little Harp, a man with a head "no larger than something
off the orange tree ... "[33] and generally "just as ugly as
it was possible to be."[34] Jamie makes unconscious reference
to himself when he tells Little Harp, "You are not the fool
I took you to be, but another fool entirely, and I ought to
break all your bones where you need them most."[35] Probably it is too much to expect of a woman that she should
make her lover see himself as a person with a head the
size of an orange. One may, on the other hand, doubt the
wisdom of a woman who goes to the opposite extreme and
makes it her business to protect a man not only from the
truth about himself but from reality of every sort. In the
scheme of values suggested by Miss Welty's fiction, recog-

nition of reality holds a very high place, and it is interesting
to see what Miss Welty envisions happening when habitual
blindness to reality collides head-on with an inescapable
stroke of fate.   That is exactly what takes place in The Ponder Heart.

       One would anticipate that the result of the collision
described above would be bathetic, and it is.   Uncle Daniel
Ponder, an advanced eccentric in his fifties, has for some
time been separated from his wife, Bonnie Dee, aged seven-
teen, who unceremoniously "ran him off" from his own house
in the country.   Finally, he has been persuaded to cut off
her allowance, and as a result she has summoned him and
his niece, Edna Earle, to a conference.   When they arrive,
simultaneously with a fierce thunder storm, Bonnie Dee is
not at all glad to see her husband.   This is hardly surprising,
as she has never shown any sign of enthusiasm for him.
However, this does not prevent Edna Earle from being en-
raged at Bonnie Dee for snubbing the man she has guarded
"heart and soul" for "a whole lifetime":

>   ... he came into the parlor all beaming pleasure
> and went shinning up to her to kiss her and she
> just jumped away when the storm went boom.   Like
> he brought it ... she just looked at him with her
> little coon eyes, and would have sent him back if
> I hadn't been there. [36]

But Uncle Daniel, in a world made safe by fantasy, shows
no awareness that he is being ignored and humiliated.   There
is a flash of lightning and burst of thunder.   Bonnie Dee
buries her face in a pillow and starts to cry.   And Uncle
Daniel, to make her stop crying, begins to tickle her ankle
with the tassel of an antimacassar.   While the storm rages
on and Bonnie Dee shrieks louder and louder, Uncle Daniel
continues to play "creep-mousie" with the tassel all the way
up to her neck and her ear,

>   with the sweetest, most forbearing smile on his
> face, a forgetful smile.   Like he forgot everything
> then that she ever did to him, how changeable she'd
> been. [37]

It turns out that Bonnie Dee is not shrieking in fear of the
storm but in reaction to the tickling.   Then she is suddenly
silent.   She has always suffered from a weak heart, and now
she has died laughing.

Faced with this bizarre horror, Uncle Daniel does nothing at all. He only sits absolutely still with his feet drawn up. All his life he has been oblivious to fatal or even threatening events:

> Oh, he hates sickness and death, will hardly come in the room with it! He can't abide funerals. [38]

He had never mentioned his father's name since the old man died. It is impossible for him to react in any positive way to a reality which demands reaction. He has avoided believing in every species of reality--money, for example. His riches, says Edna Earle,

> were all off in the clouds somewhere--like true love is, I guess, like a castle in the sky, where he could just sit and dream about it being up there for him. [39]

Safe with Edna Earle in her Beulah Hotel, he seemed quite content with being married ex officio. But now, as a ball of fire big as a man's head comes out of the fireplace, crosses the parlor, and goes out through the beaded curtains into the hall, he is right up against a reality he can neither accept nor ignore--so he faints.

Edna Earle, on the other hand, does experience the horror that unfolds with the stroke of fate. Her first reaction to the catastrophe is anger at Bonnie Dee:

> I could have shaken her for it. She'd never laughed for Uncle Daniel before in her life. And even if she had, that's not the same thing as smiling; you may think it is, but I don't. [40]

Even in retrospect, after Uncle Daniel's trial for the murder of Bonnie Dee, Edna Earle is still angry:

> ... I wished that Uncle Daniel had just whipped out and taken a stick to Bonnie Dee.... He might have picked up Grandpa's trusty old stick ... and whacked her one when she wasn't glad to see him. [41]

But Edna Earle's anger is combined with a reaction of quite another sort. It is as though she and Uncle Daniel are being mocked--mocked by the dead. When she rushes into the bathroom for ammonia, she sees herself in Bonnie Dee's mail

order magnifying mirror and gets the shock of her life:
"Edna Earle, I said, you look old as the hills!"[42] And when
she returned to the parlor, neither her momentary absence,
nor the ammonia she applies, nor the water she douses Bonnie
Dee with, nor Uncle Daniel's presence, "still as a mouse,"[43]
has the slightest effect on the laughter frozen on the dead
girl's face.

Uncle Daniel, of course, remains unchanged. Edna
Earle, who has lied at the trial about the actual circumstances of Bonnie Dee's death, will not permit Uncle Daniel,
when he rises to recount those events himself, to get beyond
a certain point, though she does have a moment of doubt:
"You don't think I betrayed him by not letting him betray
himself, do you?"[44] Then Uncle Daniel begins giving his
entire cash assets away to the crowd in the courtroom. "By
that time," says Edna Earle, "I think that all he wanted was
our approval."[45]

VII

The psychology of feeling which is suggested in Miss
Welty's fiction deserves careful attention. It is clear that
feeling and perception of reality are closely interconnected
and that both are essential to heroic action. Uncle Daniel
does possess a capacity for strong feeling, but his almost
total ignorance of reality so badly distorts his understanding
of himself and of his relationships to others that his feelings
are, for useful purposes, null and void. His heart, as Edna
Earle repeatedly points out, is full of love, but the two women he loves--Edna Earle and Bonnie Dee--are actually
strangers to him, just as Rosamond, for all her intimacy
with Jamie, was at first a stranger to him and was obliged
to remain one until she met the problem squarely and scrub-
bed away his disguise. Uncle Daniel knows nothing about
Edna Earle except that he can depend upon her to support
and protect him. That Edna Earle herself is aware of this
comes out, with unintentional irony, in her account of her uncle's habit of appropriating other people's stories for his own:

> ... he'd tell yours and his and the Man in the
> Moon's. Not mine: he wouldn't dream I had one,
> he loves me so.... [46]

As for Bonnie Dee, her unreality for Uncle Daniel is epitomized by an incident during the trial when the Ponder heart

begins beating wildly for Bonnie Dee's sister, Johnnie Ree, who does not resemble her sibling in the least but nevertheless soon attracts a Ponder-style proposal from Uncle Daniel simply because "she's got on rags and tags"[47] of Bonnie Dee's clothing.   One is reminded of Jamie Lockhart's initial preference for Rosamond's clothes over Rosamond herself. Love of this kind is not only blind; it is autonomous.   Neither it nor the feelings associated with it requires anything more than a token object; and when this object does not respond to the love which it fortuitously inspires, the product of the impasse must be a marriage, and no marriage like Uncle Daniel's to Bonnie Dee.   "I'm sure Bonnie Dee and Uncle Daniel were as happy together as most married people,"[48] Edna Earle can say, but her thought as she passes in the line beside Bonnie Dee's coffin comes from a deeper level of her understanding: "When you saw her there, it looked like she could have loved somebody!"[49]

A Welty character ideally ill-equipped for genuine heroic action would be one deficient both in feeling and in sense of reality, and therefore all but incapable of love. As it happens, the character is not hypothetical.   She appears in Miss Welty's most recent novel, The Optimist's Daughter, and her name is Fay McKelva.

Several of Fay McKelva's qualities suggest the unreconstructed Perseus-hero to whom Miss Welty never accords heroic stature.   Among these are her vanity, her belief in the efficacy of physical force, and her allegiance to her own sovereign will.   The bluntness of Fay's sensibilities is always painfully apparent.   The immediate cause of Judge McKelva's death was her violent physical attack upon him as he lay helpless in his hospital bed.   Yielding at last to Laurel McKelva's insistence that she give the reason for that brutal act, she replies, "I was trying to scare him into living! ... I tried to make him quit his old-man foolishness."[50]   Fay combines self-pity with an ominously defiant self-sufficiency: "I haven't got anybody to count on but me, myself, and I."[51] The sentiment recalls Salome, the wicked stepmother of Rosamond, and also Gloria Renfro, although it must be said at once of Gloria that, unlike Salome and Fay, she is far from being a hopeless case of self-idolatry:

"And what's your feelings now, Miss Gloria?" cried Miss Beulah.
"They don't change!   That I'm one to myself, and nobody's kin, and my own boss ... ," she said. [52]

At first glance, this insularity may seem to resemble the poised completeness of Virgie Rainey, but the likeness is superficial. Virgie is the calm center of something far greater than herself. The only thing she fears is the experience she has from time to time of feeling herself "at some moment callous over, go opaque ... "[53] and lose touch with the realities outside as well as within herself.

For all of her blunt and corrosive self-assertion, Fay has little grasp of what is real. As Laurel observes of her, "Death in its reality passed her right over."[54] Her "own life had not taught her how to feel."[55] Such a person is not so much impervious to the horror of life as insensible of it. She is a member of "the great, interrelated family of those who never know the meaning of what has happened to them."[56] The terrible irony of those whom Medusa turns to stone is that they do not know it.

The heroic task of Laurel McKelva is to meet with Fay and to resist her--not, as she comes close to doing, by physical violence, but by finding a way at last to pity her. As Laurel recognizes, her true peril lies not in anything Fay can do to her. "For Fay was without any powers of passion or imagination in herself.... She could no more fight a feeling person than she could love him."[57] Laurel's peril lies in suffering an awful inner transformation into Fay's own likeness. When Laurel arrests the stroke of the weapon with which she intends to strike her enemy, the reason, she realizes, is that she has suddenly imagined Fay as she might once have been; "undriven, unfalsifying, unvindictive."[58] Pity for Fay's lost self, the child within her, saves Laurel at the crucial instant. At the same time, it recalls to life her own past: her husband, killed in the war, her father and her mother. "Memory," she reflects, "lived not in initial possession but in the freed hands, pardoned and freed, and in the heart that can empty but fill again, in the patterns restored by dreams."[59]

VIII

Like all of Miss Welty's novels, but with unequaled abundance, Losing Battles is supplied with landmarks of human existence: birth, marriage, death, separation, and related points of transition which mark "the lonesomeness and hilarity of survival.... [60] Within the time span covered by the action--thirty hours or so--the following events take place:

Granny Vaughn's ninetieth birthday and the family reunion
which commemorates it; the first anniversary of Grandpa
Vaughn's death; the death, wake and funeral of Banner School's
retired schoolmistress, Miss Julia Mortimer; the first day
of the school year and the début of the school's new teacher;
Jack Renfro's triumphant return from Parchman Penitentiary
and his humiliating defeats by Curly Stovall and other agents
of fate; Gloria Renfro's "second wedding day"; discovery of
the identity of the orphaned Gloria's mother; the "engagement"
of Ella Fay Renfro to Curly Stovall; the uttering by Miss
Julia Mortimer of her last words ("What was the trip for?")[61]
and by Lady May Renfro of her first ones ("What you huntin',
man?");[62] the blossoming and withering of the Renfro's night-
blooming cereus; the rising of the full moon; and a rain-storm
that ends a long season of drought.

Having equipped her story with a wealth of parallel
and contrasting events, Miss Welty, with immense virtuosity,
introduces on almost every page reference to irreconcilables
whose confrontation provides for every feeling a counter-feel-
ing, for every positive its negative, and vice versa. The
effect is that of a series of montages in which opposites stand
face to face and, on occasion, merge into mysterious accord.
To cite a few examples: the Renfros, gathered for a festive
occasion, are told by Miss Julia, as from the grave, "You're
all mourners."[63] Mrs. Moody's Buick, because it is impaled
on Uncle Nathan's inspirational sign, "Destruction Is At Hand,"
is saved from plunging over the cliff at Banner Top. Jack's
horse, reportedly long since defunct at the hands of the ren-
derer, comes into view alive and well, immediately after
Miss Julia's funeral. And Brother Bethune, who had mistakenly thought that he was to preach Miss Julia's funeral
sermon, waits for Jack and Gloria at the church, this time
mistakenly believing that he is to conduct a wedding ceremony.
Thus Losing Battles moves between Scylla and Charybdis,
"swearing everything into being, swearing everything away--
but telling it."[64]

The axis upon which Losing Battles turns, spinning
off evocative details, is the gradually unfolding life and death
of Miss Julia Mortimer, followed by a dawning sense of her
resurrection. The three moments of Miss Julia's life, which
was a single, singleminded act of heroism parceled out in
time, are re-created in the minds and emotions of her former pupils, and in this sharing they advance toward heroism
of their own, each according to his lights. Their experience
is accompanied every inch of the way by reluctance, protest

and recrimination, all aimed at Miss Julia as she lived and
now disconcertingly continues to live, beyond the grave.
The very fact that she has died restores her memory to all
who had been only too glad to put her out of mind. As Miss
Beulah points out, "the littler you wish to see of some people,
the plainer you may come to remember 'em.... Even against
your will."[65] It soon becomes apparent that Miss Julia's
spirit is indeed abroad and just as authoritarian as ever:

> "Well," said Miss Beulah, "she may be
> dead and waiting in her coffin, but she hasn't given
> up yet. I see that. Trying to regiment the re-
> union into being part of her funeral!"[66]

Miss Julia's will, read to the reunion by Judge Moody, gives
explicit instructions for the proper conduct of her funeral and
burial. It closes with the words, "And then, you fools--
mourn me!"[67]

> "If this ain't keeping after us!" Uncle
> Dolphus cried. "Following us to our graves."
> "You're following her," said Judge Moody. "[68]

And, taken in more ways than one, his remark is right.

As Miss Lexie reports, Miss Julia had told the
children on her first morning at Banner School,

> "Nothing in this world can measure up to the joy
> you'll bring me if you allow me to teach you some-
> thing."[69]

But just at the end of her days, when she is dying of neglect,
loneliness and despair, she admits in her uncompromising
way that, although she has waged a life-long battle against
ignorance, "Except in those cases that you can count off on
your fingers, I lost every battle."[70] Uncle Noah Webster
has a word for what he takes to have been her aim in teaching:

> "She thought if she mortified you long
> enough, you might have hope of turning out some-
> thing you wasn't."[71]

That is how some of her pupils felt and continue to feel.
They are not so much losers of battles as the battles that
are lost.

Not all of Miss Julia's battles, fortunately, ended in entire defeat. The rejection and neglect of Miss Julia by those who knew how much they owed her troubles the conscience of two characters in particular--Judge Moody and Gloria Renfro. Judge Moody's neglect of his old friend and sometime tutor seems originally to have been caused by his resentment of her tampering with his career. He had long put off a visit to Miss Julia. Then she wrote in desperation, summoning him; and the letter, written as it was at the cost of almost indescribable pain and difficulty, had immobilized the Judge with shame. "Men are the rankest cowards,"[72] Mrs. Moody tells him; and, if that is true of Judge Moody, he pays for it in full. He is obliged to suffer hearing every detail of Miss Julia's long ordeal, something which he calls, after all is said, "The complete and utter mortification of life!"[73] Himself now in the grip of change, he awakens fully to the horror that had opened up in Julia Mortimer's life:

> "She knew exactly who she was. And what she was. What she didn't know till she got to it was what could happen to what she was."[74]

As an austere, impartial man of law, Judge Moody had long been accustomed to deal with human misery impersonally, without emotion. Now, thanks to Miss Julia, he proves that Medusa has not robbed him of the power to feel. Of what has happened to his friend he says at last, "It could make a stone cry."[75]

Gloria, who had planned to follow in Miss Julia's footsteps, still is bridling at the determined battle waged by that lady against her decision to marry Jack and over the wounding laughter with which she greeted Gloria's announcement that, for the future, she "wanted to give all [her] teaching to one."[76] From Miss Lexie, who was Miss Julia's grudging nurse in her final days, we learn that her patient, when she "lay getting worse," daily expected Gloria to visit her:

> "First she'd say, 'Gloria Short will be here soon now. She knows it's for her own good to get here on time.' Even in bed, she'd lean close to her window, press her face to the glass even on rainy mornings, not to miss the first sight of Gloria's coming."[77]

To Aunt Cleo's question, "Where were you hiding, girl?" Gloria replies, "Hiding? I was having a baby.... That's

what I was doing, and you can die from that. "78   And Miss
Beulah has her answer ready: "You can die from anything
if you try good and hard. "79   But Gloria remains unbending.
Later, when Jack, taking the role of teacher in his turn,
urges her not to "pity anybody you could love," she does
admit that she "can think of one [she] can safely pity. "80
She means Miss Julia; and pity, at least for the present,
is the closest thing to love that Gloria can spare.

Of all the celebrants at Granny Vaughn's reunion, it
is Jack Renfro who shares most generously and most fully
in the heroic moments of Miss Julia's life.   He has none of
Gloria's resentment.   Having suffered his own enforced separation from all he loved and all that he was meant to do,
he is conditioned to understanding the anguish of another
exile:

> "Are you trying to say you could do better
> than pity her?" Gloria asked him.   "You never
> laid eyes on her. "
> "I reckon I even love her," said Jack.   "I
> heard her story. "81

In her letter to Judge Moody, Miss Julia pointed out that she
had found, even in her deepest misery, a redeeming grace:

> ... the side that gets licked gets to the truth first.
> When the battle's over, something may dawn there
> --with no help from the teacher, no help from the
> pupil, no help from the book. 82

Now Jack has confirmed Miss Julia's paradox of losing battles.
Like Miss Julia, he has lost them all--or nearly all.   And,
like her, he has gotten first to the truth.   Death has not put
an end to a lifetime of devoted teaching.   Jack has listened
to Miss Julia's story well.   However many battles he has
lost and still may lose, he has become truly a hero in the
world given us by Eudora Welty.

Notes

[1] Eudora Welty, The Ponder Heart (New York: Harcourt, Brace & World, 1954), p. 90.

[2] Eudora Welty, Losing Battles (New York: Random
House, 1970), p. 84.

[3] Eudora Welty, Delta Wedding (New York: Harcourt, Brace, 1946), p. 34.

[4] Welty, Losing Battles, p. 138.

[5] Ibid., p. 235.

[6] Eudora Welty, The Golden Apples (New York: Harcourt, Brace & World, 1949), p. 275.

[7] Ibid.   [8] Ibid.

[9] Welty, Losing Battles, p. 245.

[10] Ibid.

[11] Welty, The Golden Apples, p. 276.

[12] Ibid., p. 266.   [13] Ibid., p. 267.

[14] Eudora Welty, Delta Wedding, p. 34.

[15] Ibid., p. 188.   [16] Ibid.

[17] Ibid., p. 63.   [18] Ibid., p. 189.

[19] Ibid., p. 186.   [20] Ibid., p. 187.

[21] Ibid., pp. 221-22.

[22] Welty, Losing Battles, p. 376.

[23] Ibid., p. 109.   [24] Ibid., p. 112.

[25] Eudora Welty, The Robber Bridegroom (1942; rpt. New York: Atheneum, 1963), p. 45.

[26] Ibid., p. 74.   [27] Ibid.

[28] Ibid., p. 131.   [29] Ibid., p. 146.

[30] Ibid., p. 134.   [31] Ibid., p. 135.

[32] Ibid., p. 140.   [33] Ibid., p. 98.

[34] Ibid., p. 92.   [35] Ibid., p. 111.

[36] Welty, The Ponder Heart, p. 103.

[37] Ibid. , p. 104.   [38] Ibid. , p. 29.

[39] Ibid. , p. 35.   [40] Ibid. , p. 105.

[41] Ibid. , p. 114.   [42] Ibid. , p. 105.

[43] Ibid. , p. 106.   [44] Ibid.

[45] Ibid. , p. 110.   [46] Ibid. , p. 51.

[47] Ibid. , p. 92.   [48] Ibid. , p. 116.

[49] Ibid. , p. 57.

[50] Eudora Welty, The Optimist's Daughter (New York: Random House, 1972), p. 175.

[51] Ibid. , p. 54.

[52] Welty, Losing Battles, p. 315.

[53] Welty, The Golden Apples, p. 264.

[54] Welty, The Optimist's Daughter, p. 131.

[55] Ibid. , p. 173.   [56] Ibid. , p. 84.

[57] Ibid. , p. 178.   [58] Ibid. , p. 76.

[59] Ibid. , p. 179.

[60] Welty, Losing Battles, p. 312.

[61] Ibid. , p. 241.   [62] Ibid. , p. 368.

[63] Ibid. , p. 290.   [64] Ibid. , p. 363.

[65] Ibid. , p. 283.   [66] Ibid. , p. 292.

[67] Ibid.   [68] Ibid.

[69] Ibid. , p. 273.   [70] Ibid. , p. 298.

[71] Ibid. , p. 235.   [72] Ibid. , p. 102.

[73] Ibid. , p. 301.

[74] Ibid. , p. 306.

[75] Ibid.

[76] Ibid. , p. 250.

[77] Ibid. , p. 279.

[78] Ibid.

[79] Ibid.

[80] Ibid. , p. 361.

[81] Ibid.

[82] Ibid. , p. 298.

TIME IN THE FICTION OF EUDORA WELTY

by D. James Neault

The quest for truth and beauty in the mystery of the fleeting moment serves as a thematic focus in much of Eudora Welty's fiction.   But her concern is not the historical effect or the social consciousness that evolves from a continuum of time's changes.   Miss Welty is concerned instead with the individual perception of the passing moment, the interaction of a single consciousness with each unique moment of passing time.   Miss Welty has written that "perhaps time, unpleaded with, does stand still"; and only "when a human being becomes still can all the impressions that surround him in place and time and memory--some fulfilled, some never fulfilled, but projected in dreams-- ... enter his soul then and saturate it with their full original powers.... "[1]   Thus truth and beauty, "pervading mysteries" of human life, can be perceived only in the "still moment" suspended in time.   "Indeed, as soon as the least of us stands still, that is the moment something extraordinary is seen going on in the world. "[2]

Nowhere in the writings of Eudora Welty is there an explicit definition of time; but Miss Welty's assertion that life be realized in the "present moment,"[3] or in the "here and now, or the past made here and now, "[4] suggests that her concept of time more closely resembles the "eternal now" of Tillich than la durée intérieure of Bergson.   Bergson rejects the concept of an ever-renewable moment of present time: "For our duration is not merely one instant replacing another; if it were, there would never be anything but the present--no prolonging of the past into the actual, no evolution, no concrete duration. "[5]   Tillich, like Bergson, is aware that a particulate configuration of time precludes the possibility of a "never-ending flux of time;" consequently, the riddle of the temporal "now" would remain a mystery if it were not to be comprehended in the eternal:

> The mystery is that we <u>have</u> a present; and
> even more that we have <u>our</u> future also because we
> anticipate it in the <u>present;</u> and that we have <u>our</u>
> past also, because we remember it in the <u>present</u>
> .... The riddle of the present is the deepest of
> all the riddles of time. Again, there is no answer
> except from that which comprises all time and lies
> beyond it--the eternal. Whenever we say "now" or
> "today," we stop the flux of time for us. We ac-
> cept the present and do not care that it is gone in
> the moment that we accept it. We live in it and
> it is renewed for us in every new "present." This
> is possible because every moment of time reaches
> into the eternal. 6

The question of temporal time comprehended in eternity still
leaves the nature of time shrouded in mystery. To capture
absolute time man would have to discard his finite self and
partake of the infinity that is time's essence. 7 But the mystery is not disquieting to Miss Welty, for it is in his confrontation with the "still moment" that man experiences the mystical revelation of truth and beauty.

Paradoxically, the mystery of human life resides in
man's vulnerability to time: his frailty, his uncertainty, his
mortality. The conflict that arises is between man and time
as a measurement of his mortality. This idea is best exemplified in the story "Circe," in which Miss Welty contrasts
finite man to the infinity of the supernatural. Circe, unable
to comprehend the secret of human identity, concludes that
the mystery of human life is in some way related to man's
susceptibility to time:

> I know they [men] keep something from me,
> asleep and awake. There exists a mortal mystery,
> that, if I knew where it was, I could crush like an
> island grape. Only frailty, it seems, can divine
> it--and I was not endowed with that property. They
> live by frailty! By the moment! I tell myself that
> it is only a mystery, and mystery is only uncer-
> tainty.... Yet mortals alone can divine where it
> lies in each other, can find it and prick it in all
> its peril, with an instrument of air. 8

Although all men possess in some degree the "instrument of
air"--sensitivity, imagination, inspiration, hope, love--men
are not always willing to admit to the frailty, the mortality,

that is essential to the perception of, and participation in, the passing moment of the eternal present.

The fiction of Miss Welty becomes a dramatic contrast of man's varying attitudes towards time. Virgie Rainey (The Golden Apples) best illustrates the individual who refuses to be intimidated by the apprehension of the moment; she has ignored time and has attempted to structure time, but she has never denied time. Ultimately Virgie's confrontation with life leads to the mystical revelation that hope and despair, love and separateness, growth and loss, beauty and terror, heroism and violence are inseparable and co-equal:

> Virgie never saw it differently, never doubted that all the opposites on earth were close together, love close to hate, living to dying; but of them all, hope and despair were the closest blood--unrecognizable one from the other sometimes, making moments double upon themselves, and in the doubling double again, amending but never taking back. [9]

But it is only a continuing acquiescence to the "temporal now" that leads to a final comprehension of human as well as prophetic visions of time:

> Cutting off the Medusa's head was the heroic act, perhaps, that made visible a horror in life, that was at once the horror in love, Virgie thought --the separateness. She might have seen heroism prophetically when she was young and afraid of Miss Eckhart. She might be able to see it now prophetically, but she was never a prophet. Because Virgie saw things in their time, like hearing them--and perhaps she must believe in the Medusa equally with Perseus--she saw the stroke of the sword in three moments, not one. In the three was the damnation--no, only the secret, unhurting because not caring in itself--beyond the beauty and the sword's stroke and the terror lay their existence in time--far out and endless, a constellation which the heart could read over many a night.
>   . . .
> In Virgie's reach of memory a melody softly lifted, lifted of itself. Every time Perseus struck off the Medusa's head, there was the beat of time, and the melody. Endless the Medusa, and Perseus endless. [10]

In "The Eternal Now," Tillich says that "not everybody, and nobody all the time" can ever be aware of eternity as it is manifested in the "temporal now." Virgie Rainey is perhaps the only Welty character who succeeds.

In contrast to Virgie is Cassie Morrison, through whose consciousness the identity of Virgie is revealed. Cassie "could never go for herself, never creep out on the shimmering bridge of the tree, or reach the dark magnet there that drew you inside, kept drawing you in. She could not see herself do an unknown thing."[11] And Ellen Fairchild (Delta Wedding), like Cassie Morrison, is another of Miss Welty's characters who is unable to make "the golden acquiescence ... in the present moment."[12] Ellen is not oblivious to the relationship of man to time, but she herself "never had time to sit down and fill her eyes with people and hear what they said in any civilized way."[13] Yet it is Ellen who identifies in George Fairchild the ability "of meeting a fate whose dealing out to him he would not contest...."[14] But even to Ellen, George's acceptance of life remains an inexplicable mystery:

> A feeling of uncontrollable melancholy came over her [Ellen] to see him in this half-light, which had so rested her before he came out. Dear George, whose every act could verge so closely on throwing himself away--what on earth would ever be worth that intensity with which he held it, the hurting intensity that was reflected back on him, from all passing things? ... Only George left the world she knew as pure--in spite of his fierce energies, even heresies--as he found it; still real, still bad, still fleeting and mysterious and hopelessly alluring to her.[15]

Although Ellen and Cassie, unlike George and Virgie, are incapable of action, they are both susceptible to the irrepressible attraction of the "dark magnet." Unfortunately neither is able to face the inherent danger of the unknown, the danger to which man willingly submits when he asks that time stop.

The inability to seize the moment is frequently the result of man's obsessive desire to measure time, to control time by reducing it to temporal sequence that can then be confined to a finite conceptual construct. Pirandello interprets man's desire to arrest the flux of life in fixed forms as an attempt to resist change:

> Life is a continuous flux and we seek to
> arrest it, to fix it in stable and determined forms,
> inside and outside us, because we are already fixed
> forms, forms which move in the midst of immobile
> ones and which can therefore follow the flux of life
> until, as it gradually becomes rigid, the movement,
> which has already slowed down little by little,
> ceases. The forms in ourselves by which we seek
> to arrest and fix this continuous flux are the con-
> cepts and ideals which we would like to keep con-
> sistent, all the pretenses we create, the conditions,
> the state in which we endeavor to stabilize our-
> selves. [16]

But as Mrs. Rainey observes, "Time goes like a dream no
matter how hard you run."[17] And those who attempt to fix
time in measurement will find themselves outsped.

Miss Eckhart (The Golden Apples) worships her metronome: "She kept it, like the most precious secret in the
teaching of music, in a wall safe."[18] The metronome is
symbolic of Miss Eckhart's attempted tyranny over time and
is accepted passively by her pupils who view its ticking in
their face as a part of the unpleasantness of the lesson.
Cassie recognizes the absurdity of the safe as a place of
confinement for the "infernal machine," but she does not
recognize Miss Eckhart's action to be the ritualistic immo-
bilization of time. It is Virgie Rainey who finally refuses
to "play another note with that thing in her face" and asserts
her freedom from restriction by insisting that the clock be
stopped. Consequently Miss Eckhart, to whom submission
to metronomic time is an attempt to avoid frustration and
suffering by the ordering of existence, is made vulnerable
by her involuntary confrontation with the reality of the moment. Miss Eckhart's decline is rapid, and she soon goes
"down out of sight," probably as a charity case, at the
County Farm. In her final disappointment, Miss Eckhart
returns to Morgana to destroy the MacLain house, her studio,
piano, metronome--all that had once been dear to her. But
she is unsuccessful; and with the metronome forcibly taken
from her, Miss Eckhart, "about to be touched, prodded, any
minute, but not worrying about it," stands defenseless before
the mystery of the moment.[19]

Solomon in "Livvie" also clings to an instrument of
time, his watch:

He might be dreaming of what time it was, for

> even through his sleep he kept track of it like a
> clock, and knew how much of it went by, and waked
> up knowing where the hands were even before he
> consulted the silver watch that he never let go.
> He would sleep with the watch in his palm, and
> even holding it to his cheek like a child that loves
> a plaything. 20

Solomon, by confining time, has managed to order his existence and to hold the reality of the world at bay, but "he had
built a lonely house, the way he would make a cage...."21
Solomon has succeeded in preserving his home from the violence, despair, and destruction that characterize change in
time; he has also excluded the mysterious beauty that can
be found only in confrontation with the real world. Time
catches up: death comes, and the present intrudes as Livvie
steps into "the bursting light of spring."

The examples cited thus far have been characters who,
as individuals, have recognized their relationship to time,
although they have responded differently to it. Equally important to Miss Welty's fiction are those characters who, by
participation in the social community, deny time and thus
isolate themselves from the consciousness of change and
mortality.

Circe's inability to divine the mystery of human identity is doubly painful to her when she realizes that man is
unwilling to admit to the mortality, the frailty, the capacity
for grief that is essential to its perception: "Ever since the
morning Time came and sat on the world, men have been on
the run as fast as they can go, with beauty flung over their
shoulders."22 She also recognizes man's dependence upon
"a story," but she does not associate the story with man's
attempts to deny time. Mythic ritual, derived from story,
observed by man as a denial of time and mortality, is a
common motif in the fiction of Miss Welty, but nowhere is
it better illustrated than in Delta Wedding:

> Shelley could only think in her anger of the con-
> vincing performance Troy had given as an overseer
> born and bred. Suppose a real Deltan, a planter,
> were no more real than that. Suppose a real Del-
> tan only imitated another Deltan. Suppose the be-
> havior of all men were actually no more than this
> --imitation of other men. But it had previously
> occurred to her that Troy was trying to imitate

> her father. (Suppose her father imitated ... oh,
> not he!) Then all men could not know any too well
> what they were doing. Everybody always said
> George was a second Denis. [23]

The Fairchild family, secure within the walls of Shellmound,
has insulated itself against time and uncertainty by keeping
the past alive to the exclusion of the present. The most
recent addition to the "pantheon of Fallen Fairchilds" is the
recently deceased Uncle Denis, who in life was described as
having looked like "a Greek God." Uncle George is becoming
a legend in his own time without the required death, and
Troy, who is an outsider from the hills and does not fit the
Fairchild mold, has effortlessly assumed the stature of an
overseer. Fearful of counterfeit legends, Shelley begins to
question the efficacy of any legend and suspects that the Fairchild men (probably no longer content with the slow evolution
of historical myth) have begun to enact mythic roles that they
have created for themselves.

Shelley's concern foreshadows the inevitable encroach-
ment of time upon life at Shellmound, but it also illustrates
the dichotomy of identity that underlies the social community
organized to ward off the uncontrollable forces of human existence. As a family the Fairchilds commune with their ances-
tors who look down from the walls of Shellmound; they share
their legends of the past; they participate in their weddings,
parties, funerals. As a group they are able to deny time
and to ignore mortality; as individuals they are lonely, private people. "We never wanted to be smart, one by one,"
Shelley confesses to her diary, "but all together we have a
wall, we are self-sufficient against people that come knocking,
we are solid to the outside. Does the world suspect? that
we are all very private people? I think one by one we're
all more lonely than private and more lonely than self-sufficient."[24] Shelley has begun to question if the end justifies
the means: as social identity and consciousness grow, the
private identity is forced to retreat into ever-deepening loneliness.

Like the Fairchilds, the Renfro-Beecham family of
Losing Battles also keeps the past alive by ritual and legend
that preserve the family identity and stay the forces of time
and change. The need of the Renfros and the Beechams to
fix the family identity in legend is characterized by the same
impatience that Shelley recognizes in the roles assumed by
the Fairchild men. Jack Renfro, just released from prison,

is returning home to celebrate the family reunion and the
ninetieth birthday of his mother's great grandmother Vaughn.
Cleo, a newcomer to the family by her marriage to Jack's
uncle Noah Webster Beecham, is impatient to learn the identity of Jack and the reason for his welcome:

> "I guess," said the new Aunt Cleo, "I guess
> I'm waiting for somebody to tell me what the wel-
> come for Jack Renfro is all about! What's he done
> that's so much more than all these big grown uncles
> and boy cousins or even his cripple daddy ever done?
> When did he leave home, and if he ain't let you
> have a card from him, what makes you so sure
> he's coming back today?"
>
> . . .
>
> "If you don't know nothing to start with, I
> don't reckon we could tell you all that in a hundred
> years, Sister Cleo," said Aunt Birdie. "I'm scared
> Jack'd get here before we was through."
>
> . . .
>
> "Can't she [Cleo] wait till Brother Bethune
> gets here for dinner and tells it to us all at the
> table? Surely he'll weave it into the family history
> [italics my own]," pleaded Aunt Beck. 25

The return of Jack is imminent, still in the future, but the
homecoming is anticipated in the past of the family history,
in legend, rather than in the reality of the present moment.
Ironically, Cleo (Clio) is the Muse of history, and her appearance as a newcomer into the family foreshadows a new
perspective in the apprehension of time.

Time might mistakenly be conceived as passive to the
desire of man either to accept or to deny it. But Miss
Welty's time is an inexorable, implacable force; her fiction
suggests the inevitability of the intruding present. Death,
violence, destruction--the hallmarks of time--are intruding
upon the cloistered existence of the Fairchilds. Troy, the
outsider from the hills, is moving into Marmion. George
is threatening to return and to oust his sisters from the
Grove; heretically, he intends to replace the traditional dairy
herd and cotton with fruit trees, vegetables, and cattle. And
Aunt Primrose reveals that "there are rats at the Grove,"
rats symbolic of the corrosive effects of change that is soon
to sweep the Fairchild family into the present. The eminence
of time and change is less explicit in Losing Battles, but it
is in Losing Battles that Miss Welty makes one of her rare

intrusions into her fiction as the omniscient author to record
the inevitability of movement in time despite man's efforts
to retard the flux of life:

> As they sang, the tree over them, Billy
> Vaughn's Switch with its ever-spinning leaves all
> light points at this hour, looked bright as a river,
> and the tables might have been a little train of
> barges it was carrying with it, moving slowly down-
> stream. Brother Bethune's gun, still resting
> against the truck, was travelling too, and nothing
> at all was immovable, or empowered to hold the
> scene still fixed or stake the reunion there. [26]

Miss Welty does not suggest, however, that suspension
in the present moment eliminate the past or the future. The
"still moment" should encompass "all the impressions that
surround the individual ... in place and time and memory,"
merging all past and present and future into an "eternal now."
Joel in "First Love" comes to realize that "if love does a
secret thing always, it is to reach backward, to a time that
could not be known--for it makes a history of the sorrow
and the dream it has contemplated in some instant of recognition. [27] Phoebe in "Asphodel" laughs aloud, knowing that
the picnic will never be "set rudely in the past," but will
endure forever in the "intoxicating present, still the phenomenon, the golden day." [28] It remains to the future to reveal
to Dewey of "Ladies in Spring" the final understanding that
he has interrupted a pre-arranged meeting between his father
and Opal Purcell. And even little Josie in "The Winds"
realizes the inextricability of past and future from the awareness of the moment:

> Josie lay still as an animal, and in panic
> thought of the future ... the sharp day when she
> would come running out of the field holding the
> ragged stems of the quick-picked goldenrod and
> the warm flowers thrust out for somebody. The
> future was herself bringing presents, the season
> of gifts. . . . If they would bring the time around
> once more, she would lose nothing that was given,
> she would hoard the nuts like a squirrel.
> For the first time in her life she thought,
> might the same wonders never come again? [29]

The fusion of past, present, and future causes Nina Stark
(The Golden Apples) to wonder if time is even moving:

> Nina had spotted three little shells in the sand she
> wanted to pick up when she could. And suddenly
> this seemed to her one of those movements out of
> the future, just as she had found one small brief
> one out of the past; this was far ahead of her--pick-
> ing up the shells, one, another, another, without
> time moving anymore, and Easter abandoned on a
> little edifice, beyond dying and beyond being remem-
> bered about. [30]

And in "The Burning," the time-narrative that is revealed
through the consciousness of the disoriented and hallucinated
Delilah is completely dislocated in time.

The dislocation of time is deliberate. In "Short Stories," Miss Welty expresses her admiration for D. H.
Lawrence, who disrupts chronology to "enter the magical
world of pure sense, of evocation"; and for Faulkner, who
refuses "to confine the story to its proper time sequence
... whole time bulges at the cracks to get in to the present-
time of the story." [31] She believes that art is of value only
as it is able to convey the all-emcompassing timelessness of
the "temporal now":

> ... the novel from the start has been bound up in
> the local, the "real," the present, the ordinary
> day-to-day of human experience. Where the imag-
> ination comes in is in directing the use of all this.
> That use is endless, and there are only four words,
> of all the millions that we've hatched, that a novel
> rules out: "Once upon a time." They make a
> story a fairy tale by the simple sweep of the re-
> move--by abolishing the present and the place
> where we are instead of conveying them to us.
> Of course we shall have some sort of fairy tale
> with us always--just now it is the historical novel.
> Fiction is properly at work on the here and now,
> or the past made here and now; for in novels we
> have to be there. [32]

The techniques that Miss Welty employs to create in
fiction a "still moment" that is perceived in the eternal
present are in the tradition of Flaubert, Bergson, Proust,
Joyce, and Faulkner; the use to which Miss Welty directs
those techniques is individual:

1. Myth and Mythic Allusion

Miss Welty's use of myth and mythic allusion ranges
from the explicit use of the Circe episode of The Odyssey
to the more tenuous allusion to Dionysian fertility rites in
"The Wide Net." Even a story such as "The Bride of the
Innisfallen," apparently free from mythic allusion (aside
from that imparted to it by its title), is suggestive of an
odyssey, a physical as well as metaphysical search. By
the use of myth, Miss Welty succeeds in coalescing all time
into the present of the story so as to symbolically unite dis-
parate chronological periods; and by rendering symbolic character in myth-related backgrounds, she is able to make them
timeless. Thus, as suggested by Albert J. Griffith, "Asphodel"
can become the fall of Rome, the decline of Greece, the
death of the South--any period of man's history that placed
convention above individual freedom.[33] Equally important,
however, is that Miss Welty's stories do not succeed or fail
on the credibility or acceptance of the allusion; it can be
seriously questioned if Miss Welty does suggest in "Asphodel"
the fall of Rome, Greece, or the South without seriously im-
pairing an enjoyment of the story of a small Southern community (fixed in place) dominated by the autocratic rule of an
embittered aristocrat who is attempting to withhold the forces
of life and time.

2. Fantasy and Dream

"The inside kind of story," Miss Welty has said,
"where the outside world is given, I'll always come back
to ... for the interior world is endlessly new, mysterious,
and alluring."[34] In Miss Welty's exploration of the inner
world, clear distinctions between fact and fantasy dissolve;
the impression that evolves is that of the dream, a moment
out of time in which past, present, and future are inter-
mingled and freed from the logical sequence of rational perception. Miss Welty's use of fantasy is as varied as her
use of mythic allusion. The Robber Bridegroom is her most
ambitious attempt to sustain the timeless quality of the dream.
Shortly before its publication she revealed that it was an
amalgamation of historical fact, fantasy, and fairy tale: "It
is about the Natchez Trace, and planters' beautiful daughters
and Indians and bayonets are in it--and a lifetime of fairy-
tale reading. Everything in it is something I've liked as
long as I can remember and have just now put down."[35] The
Robber Bridegroom succeeds in breaching the realm of alle-

gory and seems less satisfactory than a shorter story like
"Powerhouse," in which the uncertainty centers in the question of Gypsy's life or death; or "Why I Live at the P.O.,"
in which Sister's possible paranoia conflicts with the possibility of her rational motivation.

3. Multiple Centers of Consciousness

Multiple centers of consciousness disrupt the perception
of time as chronology by eliminating the single point of view,
even that of the omniscient author, that would preserve a
rationally-devised temporal sequence. Miss Welty usually
assumes an extratemporal perspective in her fiction. Narrative is revealed by the characters themselves in random
fragments that must be reassembled by the reader into a
spatial structure upon which intuitive, rather than conceptual,
time can be imposed. Character is likewise fragmented by
the technique and is revealed in diverse moments of vision
rather than in a stream of time. The effect of Miss Welty's
novels is a sense of duration, conceived in years, that defies
rigid chronographic organization.

4. Spatialization

Miss Welty's best use of spatialized form is the scene
in The Golden Apples in which Loch Morrison, from the two
vantage points of bedroom and tree, observes the strange
activities that take place next door in the vacant MacLain
house. The point of view is shared by Loch and his sister
Cassie. The action, arranged vertically in space, occurs
on the two levels in six different loci. A less apparent example of spatialization occurs in Losing Battles as the procession of school bus-truck-Buick-mules moves from Banner
Top into Banner. In this scene, arranged horizontally, the
multiple point of view is spatialized; the action is confined
to the single locus of the parade. In both scenes the temporal sequence is destroyed; for the duration of the scene,
narrative as chronology is halted. In the scene from The
Golden Apples, Miss Welty achieves a simultaneity of action;
in Losing Battles, a simultaneity of point of view.

5. Voluntary Memory

Voluntary memory, as a means of recapturing the

past, is employed by most of the characters in Miss Welty's
fiction, but it is only in The Optimist's Daughter that Miss
Welty treats specifically of the nature of memory and its relationship to the past. For Laurel McKelva Hand the past is
"impervious, and can never be awakened." Memory, however,
is the somnambulist: "It will come back in its wounds from
across the world ... calling us by our names and demanding
its rightful tears. It will never be impervious." Memory
is the flower that blooms on the dead wood of past experience
and renders the past "vulnerable to the living moment." [36]
Voluntary memory permits a spontaneous juxtaposition of past
and present that Allen Tate suggests renders history ahistor-
ical. Moreover, every moment of the past has been impinged
upon by all that has come before and by all (including the
present) that has happened since. Thus, the apposition of
closely spaced images of the past allows an apprehension of
time that must be perceived in sensibility rather than in the
intellect. The future is of only minor significance in Miss
Welty's fiction; it is her manipulation of past and present that
elevates her story to the region of the timeless.

6. Involuntary Memory

Certain memories become so much a part of the individual's inner world that they lie dormant within him, impervious
to all time. A sensory perception accomplishes an evocation
of that past, within the present moment, that cannot be accomplished by the conscious intelligence or voluntary memory.
The opening phrase of Für Elise rewakens in Cassie Morrison
a memory of "June Recital," and "like a wave, the gathering
past came right up to her."[37] Ellen Fairchild hears the
"whistle of flight" of the bird that has entered Shellmound,
and "dimly there seemed to be again in her life a bell clang-
ing trouble, startling at the Grove, then at their place, the
dogs beginning to clamour, the Negroes storming the back
door crying, and the great rush out of this room, like the
time there was a fire at the gin."[38] Dicey in "Kin" catches
sight of a stereopticon lying on a barrel, and she is trans-
ported backward in time "to Sunday and to Summertime" at
Mingo.[39] Proust considered the time thus remembered in-
voluntarily to be le temps souverain since it represents time
of the soul, qualitative, of no particular epoch, beyond the
deliberate jurisdiction of reason.

Art becomes for Miss Welty the medium by which
man can apprehend the reality of human life within the

eternity of the "here and now." Art, especially music, endows man with an ability to accept a knowledge of time and the real world; yet those who do confront the mystery of the moment are led ultimately, like Virgie Rainey, to the vision of the "horror in life, that was at once the horror in love ... the separateness."[40] Louis Rubin suggests that "the fortunate inhabitants of the Welty universe are those who can stay at home and manage to divert themselves in society, thus keeping out of their consciousness the knowledge of their human plight."[41] Miss Welty would admit that to those who will face reality the world is appalling, but it is only in the confrontation of the appalling that beauty is likewise revealed. If man can choose whether he accept time or deny it, Miss Welty insists that the choice rest with the individual:

> The ordinary novelist does not argue; he hopes to show, to disclose. His persuasions are all toward allowing the reader to see and hear something for himself.
> Great fiction ... abounds in what makes for confusion; it generates it, being on a scale which copies life, which it confronts. It is seldom very neat ... is capable of contradicting itself, and is not impervious to humor. There is absolutely everything in great fiction but a clear answer. [42]

Notes

[1] Eudora Welty, "Some Notes on River Country," Harper's Bazaar, No. 2786 (Feb. 1944), p. 156.

[2] Welty, "Place in Fiction," South Atlantic Quarterly, LV (Jan. 1956), 63.

[3] Welty, "Must the Novelist Crusade?" reprinted in Borzoi College Reader, 2nd ed. (New York: Knopf, 1971), p. 703.

[4] Welty, "Place in Fiction," p. 58.

[5] Henri Bergson, Creative Evolution (New York: Random House, 1944), pp. 6-7.

[6] Paul Tillich, "The Eternal Now," in The Eternal Now (New York: Scribners, 1963), pp. 130-131.

[7]See Margaret Mein, Proust's Challenge to Time (Manchester: University Press, 1962), p. 5. Even Tillich suggests that "not everybody, and nobody all the time, is aware of the 'eternal now' in the temporal 'now'."

[8]Welty, "Circe," in The Bride of the Innisfallen (New York: Harcourt, Brace and World, 1955), pp. 105-106.

[9]Welty, The Golden Apples (New York: Harcourt, Brace and World, 1949), p. 265.

[10]Ibid., pp. 275-276. [11]Ibid., p. 77.

[12]Welty, Delta Wedding (New York: Harcourt, Brace and World, 1946), p. 222.

[13]Ibid., p. 221.   [14]Ibid., p. 221.

[15]Ibid., p. 80.

[16]Luigi Pirandello, Umorismo, tr. Caputi, reprinted in Modern Drama (New York: Knopf, 1966), p. 474.

[17]The Golden Apples, p. 9.

[18]Ibid., p. 45.   [19]Ibid., p. 88.

[20]Welty, "Livvie" in The Wide Net (New York: Harcourt, Brace and World, 1943), pp. 162-163.

[21]Ibid., p. 173.

[22]"Circe," p. 108.

[23]Delta Wedding, p. 186.

[24]Ibid., p. 84.

[25]Welty, Losing Battles (New York: Random House, 1970), p. 21.

[26]Ibid., p. 223.

[27]Welty, "First Love" in The Wide Net, p. 28.

[28]Welty, "Asphodel" in The Wide Net, p. 115.

[29] Welty, "The Winds" in The Wide Net, p. 134.

[30] The Golden Apples, p. 151.

[31] Welty, "Short Stories," Atlantic Monthly, CLXXXIII (Feb.-Mar., 1949), pp. 48-49.

[32] "Place in Fiction," p. 58.

[33] Albert J. Griffith, Eudora Welty's Fiction, unpub. diss., Univ. of Texas, 1959, p. 33.

[34] Welty quoted by Bernard Kalb, "The Author," Saturday Review, XXXVIII (April 9, 1955), p. 18.

[35] Robert Van Gelder, "An Interview with Eudora Welty," in Writers and Writing (New York: Scribners, 1946), p. 288.

[36] Welty, The Optimist's Daughter (New York: Random House, 1972), pp. 115, 179.

[37] The Golden Apples, p. 37.

[38] Delta Wedding, p. 162.

[39] Welty, "Kin" in The Bride of the Innisfallen, p. 140.

[40] The Golden Apples, p. 275.

[41] Louis Rubin, "The Golden Apples of the Sun," in The Faraway Country (Seattle: University of Washington Press, 1963), p. 151.

[42] "Must the Novelist Crusade?" p. 703.

THE POETICS OF PROSE:
Eudora Welty's Literary Theory

by Albert J. Griffith

The methodology of fiction, Eudora Welty once observed, is a "blessedly open question." "The artist at work
functions," she noted, "while whoever likes to may explain
how he does it (or failing that, why)--without, however, the
least power of prevention or prophecy or even cure. "[1]

The "how" and "why" of Eudora Welty at work have
indeed been explored by many critics, without any very
notable accomplishments in the way of explanation. The
critics have, too often, tended to dichotomize her style and
her substance, often lauding the lavishness of the former
while deploring the deficiencies of the latter. Her fellow
novelist Hamilton Basso has put it bluntly: "Miss Welty,
generally speaking, is most frequently praised because she
can write. There's no doubt about that. She can do things
with the English language that have all the unpredictable
wonder and surprise of a ball of mercury rolling about in
the palm of one's hand. But the point, it seems to me, is
not whether Miss Welty can write but what she has done
with her writing. "[2]

And it is this question--"what has she done with her
writing"--that has caused the critics, especially her early
ones, the greatest consternation. Isaac Rosenfield, for
instance, complained of self-conscious "artiness," "a desperate, dead-end estheticism," "a poetry of textures that
are never felt, of glass leaves and glass birds." Time
found that her "flashing, strange stories" were "about as
human as a fish," noting a "delicateness of sensibility which
borders at once on genius and indecency." The Times Literary Supplement found that her "bold and individual talent"
quickly began "to overreach itself." Lionel Trilling thought

51

that nothing could be "falser, more purple and 'literary'" than her "conscious simplicity." "Miss Welty is being playful and that is perfectly all right," Trilling said, "but she is also aware of how playful she is and that is wearisome." Even as late as The Bride of the Innisfallen, one critic was lamenting the "quicksand of whimsy" and another the "preciousness" and "fragile, verbose and hypersensitive" femininity of her prose. Throughout her career, critics have complained about her "needless ambiguity," her "over-indulgence" in the fashionable use of myth, and her "unnecessarily indirect and self-consciously elliptical" use of "obscure or undecipherable symbol."[3]

Perhaps Diana Trilling developed the case against Miss Welty most cogently in a contemporary review of The Wide Net, when she argued that Miss Welty had "developed her technical virtuosity to the point where it outweighs the uses to which it is put." "The stories themselves," she said, "stay with their narrative no more than a dance, say, stays with its argument." She added:

> Now I happen to think that to make a ballet out of words is a perversion of their best function, and I dislike--because it breeds exhibitionism and insincerity--the attitude toward narrative which allows an author to sacrifice the precise meaning of language to its rhythms and patterns.... When an author says "Look at me" instead of "look at it," there is insincerity, as I see it.... Miss Welty's prose constantly calls attention to herself and away from the object. ... she is not only being falsely poetic, she is being untrue.[4]

It was Robert Penn Warren who first exposed the premises of this kind of critical judgment. The indictment, he noted, does not treat primarily of "failures to fulfill the object the artist has set herself but of the nature of that object." The disparagment of the critic, he suggested, may result from the perceived discrepancy between the work of art under consideration and some "abstract definition" or "formalistic conception" of genre in the mind of the critic. "The critic denies, in effect, that Miss Welty's present kind of fiction is fiction at all," Warren observed, and the condemnation is apparently based on the failure of Miss Welty's works to fit the anticipated conventions of a preconceived genre.[5]

What Warren grasped from the evidence of the stories themselves--that Eudora Welty was redefining the genre in which she worked--is now fully supported by the ample body of literary theory which Miss Welty has published in the intervening years. She has made it clear from the beginning that she dreams only of having her fiction evaluated on its own terms:

> It seems to me too almost the first hope we ever had, when we gave someone a story all fresh and new, was that the story would read new. And that's how we should read.
> What bliss! Think how often this is denied us. That's why we think of childhood books so lovingly. But hasn't every writer the rightful wish to have his story so read? And isn't this wish implicit in the story itself? By reading second-handedly, or obediently as taught, or by approaching a story without an open mind, we wrong its very first attribute--its uniqueness, with its sister attribute of freshness. We are getting to be old, jaded readers--instructed, advised readers, victims of summaries and textbooks and if we write stories as victims of this attitude ourselves, what will happen to us?[6]

Miss Welty has presented her own notions about fiction as a literary form in a series of fragmentary discussions stretching over a period of some thirty years. Most of her significant ideas are contained in the slim monograph Short Stories (1949) and a half-dozen major essays, but these key treatments are supplemented and reinforced by more ephemeral comments in interviews, journalistic articles, and book reviews. Collectively, these pieces reveal a well developed and fairly consistent set of concepts and principles defining the genre of fiction as she understands and practices it. If her ideas are reorganized according to the three-fold criteria of model, means, and manner which Aristotle used in his Poetics for the differentiation of literary forms, it will be seen that Miss Welty pays scant attention to some of the most commonly accepted hallmarks of fiction. The elements she stresses as essential to effective fiction are, in fact, more often thought of as elements proper to lyric rather than to narrative expression.

What, according to Miss Welty's theories, is the "model" for fiction? To put it another way, what is the

object which fiction imitates? Ordinarily, we might think of
fiction as taking "man in action" as its object of imitation,
just as drama might be presumed to take "man in conflict"
and lyric poetry "man in a moment of emotion" as their proper
objects.   Such a judgment, however, involves the assumptions
that the primary technique of fiction is narration and that the
primary subject of narration is human beings in a process of
change over a period of time.   The traditional elements of
"plot" (or "incident") and "character" are the means through
which this change is revealed; "What is character," Henry
James said, "but the determination of incident?   What is
incident but the illustration of character?"   Yet it was James
who showed us that some of the traditional boundaries between fiction and drama did not hold, as he shifted his focus
from narration to "scene," which had hitherto been thought
of as the special province of drama.

Although she neglects neither narration nor scene,
Eudora Welty shifts the focus once more--as consciously
and purposefully as James shifted it in his day.   She notes
the possibilities open to the fictionist:

> We've seen that a story's major emphasis
> may fall on the things that make it up--on char-
> acter, on plot, on its physical or moral world, in
> sensory or symbolic form.   Now we see that per-
> haps the way this emphasis is let fall may deter-
> mine the value of the story.   May determine not
> how well it is written, for that is in the lap of
> other gods, but the worth of its being written.
> Of course fashion and the habits of under-
> standing stories at given periods in history may
> play their parts, unconsciously or wilfully.   But
> mainly, I venture to think, the way emphasis falls,
> the value of a story is the thing nearest dependent
> upon the individual and personal factor involved,
> the writer behind the writing. [7]

And what emphasis creates the greatest value in a story?
Well, certainly not an emphasis on traditional plot, character,
or theme.   "The fine story writers seem, have you noticed?
to be in a sense obstructionists," Miss Welty argues.   D. H.
Lawrence, for example, "refuses to get his story told, to let
his characters talk in any natural way--the story is held up
forever, and through so delaying and through such refusal
on the author's part, we enter the magical world of pure
sense, of evocation--the shortest cut known through the woods. "[8]

The shortest cut? Not straightforward narrative, not plot, not character. What then? Pure sense. Evocation. The emphasis she praises in the writers she chooses to discuss is never an emphasis on getting the story told. In Hemingway, it's "opaqueness;" in Crane, it's "kinetic pleasure;" in Mansfield and Chekhov, it's the momentary revelation of the "secret life;" in Faulkner, it's a "dilation in time-sense and intractibility in space sense."[9] Good writers, in fact, are not even primarily concerned with the story's present time:

> Katherine Anne Porter shows us that we do not have to see a story happen to know what is taking place. For all we are to know, she is not looking at it happen herself when she writes it; for her eyes are always looking through the gauze of the passing scene, not distracted by the immediate and transitory; her vision is reflective.[10]

Suspense, usually thought so crucial to narrative, does not even depend on "disclosure of the happenings of the narrative," but on "the writing of the story, which becomes one single long sustained moment for the reader."[11] Practical problems of plotting--what Miss Welty calls facetiously "the problem of How the Old Woman Got Home"--are not "truly important problems" but only "minutiae," just little nuisances to plague and absorb the writer.[12]

If plot action, then, is not of central importance to a story, what is? Miss Welty's own well-known predilection, of course, is to focus on "Place" as the center of her stories. She has devoted one whole essay to the explication of her notion of Place and she has further elaborated on the idea on numerous other occasions. Nevertheless, the concept of Place is probably the most misunderstood element in her overall literary theory, often being trivialized to mean nothing more than setting, as a chauvinistic regionalist or a sentimental local colorist might comprehend that element. Miss Welty does her best to define this "lesser angel" which watches over fiction:

> Place in fiction is the named, identified, concrete, exact and exacting, and therefore cred-ible, gathering-spot of all that's been felt, is about to be experienced, in the novel's progress. Loca-tion pertains to feeling, feeling profoundly pertains to Place; Place in history partakes of Place....

>The very notion of moving a novel brings ruder
>havoc to the mind and affections than would a cen-
>tury's alteration in its time. It's only too easy to
>conceive that a bomb that could destroy all trace
>of places as we know them, in life and through
>books, could also destroy all feelings as we know
>them, so irretrievably and so happily are recog-
>nition, memory, history, valor, love, all the in-
>stincts of poetry and praise, worship and endeavor,
>bound up in Place. [13]

The equating of fiction with Place and of Place with
feelings is, of course, an indirect identification of fiction
with feelings. Though lyric poetry would ordinarily be thought
of as the best vehicle for feelings, Miss Welty insists that
"fiction provides the ideal texture through which the feeling
and meaning that permeate our own personal, private lives
will best show through. " That texture is a result of Place
with the "mass of association--association more poetic than
actual" which is bound up with it. [14]

The feelings Miss Welty speaks of as relating to Place
seem to be those of the fictional characters and of the audience, as well as those of the writer. The characters of a
story gain their authenticity and credibility from the Place
which keeps them grounded in a physical and emotional reality; "Place, then, has the most delicate control over character too: by confining character, it defines it. " Place establishes "a chink-proof world of appearance" to link the
reader with that "initial, spontaneous, overwhelming, driving
charge of personal inner feeling that was the novel's first
reason for being. "[15] The writer, Miss Welty seems to say,
uses Place as an objective correlative for his own passion:

>Taking a particular situation existing in his
>world, and what he feels about it in his own breast
>and what he can make of it in his head, he con-
>structs on paper, little by little, an equivalent of
>it. Literally it may correspond to a high degree
>or to none at all; emotionally it corresponds as
>closely as he can make it. [16]

Furthermore, she seems to believe that the emotions of a
concrete situation can spontaneously overflow into Weltian
prose just as readily as into Wordsworthian verse:

>Like a good many other writers, I am my-
>self touched off by place. The place where I am

and the place I know, and other places that familiarity with and love for my own make strange and
lovely and enlightening to look into, are what set
me to writing stories.   To such writers I suppose
place opens a door in the mind, either spontaneously or through beating it down, attrition.   The
impression of place as revealing something is an
indelible one--which of course is not to say it
isn't highly personal and very likely distorted.
The imagination further and further informs and
populates the impression according to present
mood, intensification of feeling, beat of memory,
accretion of idea, and by the blessing of being lo-
cated--contained--a story so charged is now capable of being written. [17]

The explicit physical textures of Place finally become the
means for the transfer of emotion from the storyteller to
the audience:

And as Place has functioned between the writer and
his material, so it functions between the writer and
reader.   Location is the ground-conductor of all
the currents of emotion and belief and moral con-
viction that charge out from the story in its course.
These charges need the warm hard earth under-
foot, the light and lift of air, the stir and play of
mood, the softening bath of atmosphere that gives
the likeness-to-life that life needs.   Through the
story's translation and ordering of life, the uncon-
vincing raw material becomes the very heart's familiar.   Life is strange.   Stories hardly make it
more so; with all they are able to tell and surmise,
they make it more believably, more inevitably so. [18]

If the model of imitation for fiction is the emotional
reality of concrete human situations, as Miss Welty maintains,
then it is hardly any wonder that the "manner" of successful
fiction should be as strange and numinous as the life it mir-
rors.   Stories are not likely to have "a perfect Christmas
tree of symmetry," she says; "the reader of more willing
imagination, who has specified for something else, may find
the branchings not what he's expecting either, and the fulfillment not a perfect match, not at all to the letter of the
promise--rather to a degree (and to a degree of pleasure)
mysterious. " Against this mysteriousness, the tools of the
critic are often unavailing:

The analyst, should the story come under his eye, may miss this gentle shock and this pleasure too, for he's picked up the story at once by its heels (as if it had swallowed a button) and is examining the writing as his own process in reverse, as though a story (or any system of feeling) could be the more accessible to understanding for being hung upside down. [19]

Miss Welty's concept of mysteriousness in fiction is, perhaps, the clue both to the vagaries of her language and the nebulousness of her themes. This double element of ambiguity is purposive, intended to correspond to the equivocation of esthetic emotions, which speak both to the conscious and the subconscious mind, despite "quondam obstruction." "We are speaking of beauty," she says. "And beauty is not a blatant or promiscuous or obvious quality--indeed at her finest she is somehow associated with obstruction--with reticence of a number of kinds."[20] The first thing a reader sees in a story is this fascinating attribute of mystery. "Every good story has mystery--not the puzzle kind, but the mystery of allurement," she insists. "As we understand the story better, it's likely that the mystery does not necessarily decrease; rather it simply grows more beautiful."[21]

But Miss Welty does not make the pursuit of mystery an indiscriminating excuse for obscurity. It is true that she praises that "sense of opaqueness" found in masters of the short story like Faulkner ("Faulkner's prose, let's suspect, is intolerantly and intolerably unanalysable and quite pure ... with its motes bright-pure and dark-pure falling on us"),[22] D. H. Lawrence ("the atmosphere that cloaks D. H. Lawrence's stories is pure but thick cover, a cloak of self-luminous air"),[23] and Hemingway ("action can be inscrutable, more than sensation can ... just as voluptuous, too, just as vaporous and, as I am able to see it, much more desperately concealing").[24] Yet she can also praise Glenway Wescott because "everywhere is the dignity of a style in which there is nothing wasteful and nothing wanting in saying an explicit thing."[25] And, for affecting stylistic obscurantism inadroitly, she takes to task authors like Edita Morris ("the author seems to be writing too delicately, in order to keep her distance from such extraordinary characters, that we seem especially to notice her tiptoeing")[26] and Dorothy Baker ("her indistinct, often careless, sometimes ungrammatical sentences show a disregard for accuracy and clarity in the interest of manner and mannerism").[27] In her own stories, Miss Welty has been careful to try to merge or identify the abstract (including that desirable mysteriousness) with the concrete. She has revealed that in the reworking of "No Place for You, My Love" she cut some "odd" sentences out of it, "not because they were odd--for the story is that--but because they would tantalize some cooling explanations out of the mind if they stayed in." "I had no wish to sound mystical," she proclaims, "but I did expect to sound mysterious now and then, if I could: this was a circumstantial, realistic story in which the reality was mystery."[28]

If mystery is inherent in both the real-life model fiction imitates and in the manner of imitation, then it is not surprising to find it also in the "means" of imitation. "If this makes fiction sound full of mystery," Miss Welty says, "I think it's fuller than I know how to say." Language, of course, is fiction's means to the imitation of life, and language also is full of mystery. "In writing, do we try to solve this mystery?" she asks. "No, I think we take hold of the other end of the stick. In very practical ways, we re-discover the mystery."[29] Not for her, then, the precision and clarity of pure denotation--that is the language of the cognitive domain, the language of objectivity and detachment, the language of science. As a fiction writer, Miss Welty knows she must choose the complex language of connotation-- the language of the affective domain, the language of subjectivity and passion, the language of poetry and myth. "This very leap in the dark is exactly what writers write fiction in order to try," she contends. "My feeling is that it's when reading begins to impress on us what degrees and degrees of communication are possible between novelists and ourselves as readers that we surmise what it has meant, can mean, to write novels."[30]

Eudora Welty knows what it can mean, and she has expressed that knowledge in what amounts to a fairly complete and coherent poetics of prose. Throughout a series of declarations over some three decades, she has consistently argued that fiction, like poetry and painting, is a "system of feeling" and that the artistic choices that go into it must be appropriate to the re-creation and communication of the mystery which surrounds human emotion. If such principles make her own fiction seem remote or obscure or needlessly contrived, that is not the fault of the fiction itself but of the reader's expectations. Fiction need not be totally representational, as we have come to presume it will be; it has just as much right as a genre to be presentational--to deal with the essential inner reality even at the expense of external verisimilitude--as does lyric poetry or poetic drama. The very concreteness of Miss Welty's writing has been misleading in this respect; it has lured readers into thinking of her as a regional realist manqué, a slightly confused and obfuscating local colorist who can't quite stay on target. As her disquisitions on Place make eminently clear, however, the imagistic texture of her work is not intended to educe the quotidian surface of conventional realism but rather the heightened mystery of lyric responses.

Read as she wishes to be read, Eudora Welty is a poet who deliberately uses prose as her medium. She is bound to Place but suspended in Time, like the symbolic humming-bird which appears throughout The Golden Apples:

> He was a little emerald bobbin, suspended as always before the opening four-o'clocks. Metallic and misty together, tangible and intangible, splendid and fairylike, the haze of his invisible wings mysterious, like the ring around the moon--had anyone ever tried to catch him? ... Let him be suspended there for a moment each year for a hundred years--incredibly thirsty, greedy for every drop in every four-o'clock trumpet in the yard, as though he had them numbered--then dart. [31]

Ever suspended but ever in motion, the fiction writer, like the humming-bird, cannot be easily caught and contained, especially in the nets of our traditional expectations. "The fact that a story will reduce to elements, can be analyzed," Miss Welty observes, "does not necessarily mean it started with them, certainly not consciously." What elements produce the iridescence of the humming-bird? What elements create the numinous vision of the prose poem?

"A story," Eudora Welty says, "can start with a bird song. "[32]

Notes

[1]"How I Write," Virginia Quarterly Review, 31 (Spring, 1955), 240, 242.

[2]"Look Away, Look Away, Look Away," New Yorker, 22 (May 11, 1946), 89.

[3] Isaac Rosenfield, "Consolations of Poetry," New Republic, 109 (October 18, 1943), 525, and "Double Standard," New Republic, 114 (April 29, 1946), 633; "Sense and Sensibility," Time, 40 (September 27, 1943), 100-101; "Southern Allegory," Times Literary Supplement, January 22, 1944, p. 41; Lionel Trilling, "American Fairy Tale," Nation, 155 (December 19, 1942), 687; "Telling Stories," Times Literary Supplement, November 11, 1955, p. 669; Jean Holzhauer, "Seven Stories," Commonweal, 62 (April 29, 1955), 109-110; United States Quarterly Review, 11 (1955), 353; Francis Steegmuller, "Small Town Life," New York Times Book Review, 54 (August 21, 1949), 5; William Peden, "The Incomparable Welty," Saturday Review, 38 (April 9, 1955), 18.

[4] "Fiction in Review," Nation, 157 (October 2, 1943), 386.

[5] "The Love and the Separateness in Miss Welty," Kenyon Review, 6 (Spring 1944), 249.

[6] Short Stories (New York: Harcourt, Brace and Company, 1949), pp. 10-11.

[7] Ibid., p. 50.   [8] Ibid., pp. 50-51.

[9] Ibid., pp. 15-46.

[10] Eudora Welty, "The Eye of the Story," Yale Review, 55 (Winter, 1965), 267.

[11] Ibid., p. 270.

[12] Short Stories, p. 6.

[13] "Place in Fiction," Three Papers on Fiction (Northampton, Mass.: Smith College, 1962), p. 6.

[14] Ibid., p. 2.   [15] Ibid., pp. 6-9.

[16] "Must the Novelist Crusade?" Atlantic, 216 (October 1965), 105.

[17] "How I Write," pp. 242-243.

[18] "Place in Fiction," pp. 10-11.

[19] "How I Write," p. 244.

[20] Short Stories, p. 50.

[21] Ibid., p. 13.

[22] "In Yoknapatawpha," Hudson Review, 1 (Winter 1949), 598.

[23] Short Stories, p. 12.

[24] Ibid.

[25] "Told With Severity and Irony," New York Times Book Review, March 4, 1945, p. 18.

[26] "Find-Spun Fantasies," New York Times Book Review, February 18, 1945, p. 5.

[27] "Somnolence and Sunlight, Sound of Bells, the Pacific Surf," New York Times Book Review, August 15, 1948, p. 5.

[28] "How I Write," p. 250.

[29] "Words into Fiction," Three Papers on Fiction, p. 18.

[30] Ibid., p. 16.

[31] "June Recital," The Golden Apples (New York: Harcourt, Brace and Company, 1949), p. 59.

[32] Short Stories, p. 9.

PSYCHIC DISTANCES IN A CURTAIN OF GREEN:
Artistic Successes and Personal Failures

by Barbara Fialkowski

In her introduction to Eudora Welty's A Curtain of
Green, Katherine Anne Porter admits:

> a deeply personal preference for this particular
> kind of story, where external act and the internal
> voiceless life of the human imagination almost meet
> and mingle on the mysterious threshold between
> dream and waking, one reality refusing to admit
> or confirm the existence of the other, yet both
> conspiring toward the same end.

One might suppose the curtain of green a separation between
the inner and outer worlds of Welty's characters. If Welty
parts that curtain, pulls it abruptly aside, the worlds of fantasy and reality fuse.

In the title story, "A Curtain of Green," Welty describes the inner, despairing life of Mrs. Larkin,

> But memory tightened about her easily, without any
> prelude of warning or even despair. She would see
> promptly, as if a curtain had been jerked quite un-
> ceremoniously away from a little scene, the front
> porch of the white house, the shady street in front,
> and the blue automobile in which her husband ap-
> proached, driving home from work.

Welty gives us that shadowy mid-ground territory that
Nathaniel Hawthorne spoke of "somewhere between the real
world and fairey land where the Actual and the Imaginary may
meet and each imbue itself with the nature of the other."

The results are somewhat paradoxical for both Welty

and Hawthorne. If the central character himself is incapable
of distinguishing between the private and public world, he
gets swallowed in a miasma of solipsism. Such is the life
of poor Mr. Marblehall, thinking his exploits so outrageous
"that if people knew about his double life, they'd die." However, in reality, "nobody gives a hoot about any old Mr.
Marblehall. He could die for all they care; some people
even say, 'Oh, is he still alive?'"

These are stories of interiors, of people cut off from
the real world. In "The Whistle," Jason and Sara Morton

> Lay trembling with cold, but no more communica-
> tion in their misery than a pair of window shutters
> beaten by a storm.

In "The Key," Ellie and Albert Morgan's communication with
the outside world is shut off by the very physical reality of
their deafness. However, communication between the two of
them is just as stilted. As Welty suggests, finally there
must exist a

> proper separation that lies between a man and a
> woman, the thing that makes them what they are
> in themselves, their secret life, their memory of
> the past, their childhood, their dreams.

Such separation may be proper, but often results in
isolation and disaster. Clytie's isolation is symbolized by
her "nearsighted way" of "peering ahead" and the big old
house she kept herself hidden in. Her isolation is the direct
result of her sister Octavia, a woman who believed an open
window a hazard, "Rain and sun signified ruin in Octavia's
mind. Going over the whole house, Clytie made sure that
everything was safe." Significantly, Clytie became her sister's spokesman. When Octavia "let the curtain drop at last,
Clytie would be left there speechless."

Her loss of self has been complete. Whether the
self is too large or too small, the self is undefined: "Clytie
swayed a little and looked into the slightly moving water.
She thought she saw a face there." The face was her own,
but for Clytie, unfamiliar: "It was the face she had been
looking for, and from which she had been separated." She
discovered in that face "signs of waiting, of suffering." If
the world was indistinguishable from the self, and Clytie was
drowning in the world, then the self was indistinguishable
from the world and

Clytie did the only thing she could think of to do.
She bent her angular body further, and thrust her
head into the barrel, under the water, through its
glittering surface into the kind, featureless depth,
and held it there.

The final image of Clytie is selfless, "her poor ladylike
blackstockinged legs up-ended and hung apart like a pair of
tongs."

One might view Mrs. Larkin's garden as a similar
psychic extension: "To a certain extent, she seemed not to
seek for order, but to allow an overflowering, as if she consciously ventured forever a little farther, a little deeper,
into her life in the garden." Even Bowman, in "Death of a
Traveling Salesman," has a desire or, perhaps compulsion,
to see the world as an extension of his own rootlessness and
his own loneliness. Perhaps, the symbols altered a bit, the
stories are the same.

Traveling is Bowman's distance from humanity, his
escape, finally, from himself. His sickness is as psychic
as it is physical and the implication is that it is a disease
of the heart. Welty gradually parts the curtain before him
and Bowman discovers that the old woman is young, the boy
is her husband and not her son, and their home together is
fruitful and not barren:

There was nothing remote or mysterious here--only
something private. The only secret was the ancient
communication between two people. But the memory
of the woman's waiting silently by the cold hearth,
of the man's stubborn journey a mile away to get
fire, and how they finally brought out their food and
drink and filled the room proudly with all they had
to show, was suddenly too clear and too enormous
within him for response....

Bowman discovered here, at the end of the road, the very
thing he has spent a lifetime running from and believing could
not exist: "Bowman could not speak. He was shocked with
knowing what was really in this house. A marriage, a fruitful marriage."

The discovery is overwhelming. Taking his bags,
Bowman runs from the house. "Just as he reached the road,
where his car seemed to sit in the moonlight like a boat, his
heart gave off tremendous explosions like a rifle, bang bang

bang. " If Mr. Marblehall wrongly thought that his living
fantasy would have a far-reaching effect on humanity, so
Bowman mistakenly felt his disease a pervasive one: "He
covered his heart with both hands to keep anyone from hearing
the noise it made. But nobody heard it. "

Mr. Marblehall, R. J. Bowman, Clytie, Jason and
Sara Morton and Ellie and Albert Morgan all suffer from
their isolation. Whether this isolation is socially imposed
or blindly self-imposed, finally, does not matter. It is a disease
of the human condition that must be recognized. Welty allows
us but a momentary glimpse of the interminglings of their
fantasies and realities.

Exactly half way through A Curtain of Green, we come
across a story entitled "A Memory" in which it is hinted that
the artist, too, is isolated from humanity. The implication
is that such an isolated condition is an artistic necessity.
As Katherine Anne Porter suggests,

> there might be something of early personal history
> in the story of a child on the beach, alienated from
> the world of adult knowledge by her state of child-
> hood, who hoped to learn the secrets of life by
> looking at everything, squaring her hands before
> her eyes to bring the observed thing into a frame--
> the gesture of one born to select, to arrange, to
> bring apparently disparate elements into harmony
> within deliberately fixed boundaries.

Porter finds the power of such objectivity "admirable," but
one must wonder about the sanity of a child who faints at
the intrusion of an uncontrolled reality.

Objectivity is, as Porter suggests, a necessary pre-
requisite for an artist. Henry James might refer to objectivity as the ability to survey the whole field. But that ability is to survey the whole field. That is the artist's moral
obligation, not to be overwhelmed by the world, but to include its disparities. Exclusion should be a matter of artistic judgment and not one of personal taste. One might compare the narrator's final retreat in "A Memory" to the positive though paradoxically useless action of the red-haired
young man in "The Key. "

While painting or framing is the artistic metaphor in
"A Memory," embroidery is that metaphor in "The Key,"

"You could hear their embroidering movements in the weeds outside, which somehow gave the effect of some tenuous voice in the night telling a story." Ellie and Albert Morgan arrive at the station "touched here and there with a fine yellow dust, like finger marks." The red-haired young man stands aside watching these two

> in compassion, in making any intuitive present or sacrifice, or in any way of action at all--not because there was too much in the world demanding all his strength, but because he was too deeply aware. [italics mine]

The complete observer, "He had seen the dust on her throat and a needle stuck in her collar where'd she'd forgotten it, with a thread running through the eye--the final details."

The young man must embroider the facts of the story from these details; his eye is a needle. Welty does not imply that such objectivity is without its scars. After all, what is the artist's moral obligation to the field he surveys? Understanding the crisis of emptiness that Ellie and Albert face, the red-haired young man can offer what? The key was itself an accidental gift, at least the key that Albert picks up. However, the key the young man offers Ellie is an attempt at intrusion based on artistic understanding. "The Key" ends with this intrusion,

> and in his eyes, all at once wild and searching, there was certainly, besides the simple compassion in his regard, a look both restless and weary, very much used to the comic. You could see that he despised and saw the uselessness of the thing he had done.

Hawthorne faced a similar crisis in the depiction of his artist figures. They were often guilty of the same flaw as his villains. The question is, at what point does compassion become cold observation? One may think of old Rappacini or Ethan Brand to sense Hawthorne's dilemma. Finally one must believe that it is this paradox that provides the source of artistic flow. The loneliness of distance and the technique derived of detachment combine in the artistic creation.

Loneliness implies the involvement of the heart. Detachment by itself is villainous and we slip toward that villainy in "A Memory." The artist/narrator recollects her

life as a young girl approaching adolescence. She preferred
her world motionless, "a few solitary people in fixed posi-
tions." Unlike the red-haired young man, she did not view
the world with compassion: "Ever since I had begun taking
painting lessons, I had made small frames with my fingers,
to look out at everything." She found the lives of the old
people she saw at the beach "consciously of no worth to
anything."

The Welty narrator notes, "I was at an age when I
formed a judgment upon every person and every event which
came under my eye, although I was easily frightened." The
child is afraid of being overwhelmed by the world at large.
"When a person, or a happening, seemed to me not in keeping with my opinion, or even my hope or expectation, I was
terrified by a vision of abandonment and wildness which tore
my heart with a kind of sorrow."

Terrified of reality, the child distanced or isolated
herself from its community, thus intensifying her ability or
need to observe:

> It did not matter to me what I looked at; from any
> observation I would conclude that a secret life had
> been nearly revealed to me--for I was obsessed
> with notions about concealment, and from the smallest
> gesture of a stranger I would wrest what was to me
> a communication or a presentiment.

The central words here are "to me," because such
isolation from the world had led to a double life: "Through
some intensity I had come almost into a dual life, as observer and dreamer." This is a story of adolescence, for
the young girl is in love from a distance with a young boy
in her class. She had touched his wrist and the touch carried a weight that would have to be called Jamesian, an "encounter which we endured on the stairs," and which became
a moment of "overwhelming beauty."

Such beauty is endangered and just as the young girl
feared motion, change and reality, she feared this beauty.
It left her unprepared for the inevitable violent intrusion of
reality--an intrusion that took the form of a nosebleed, something that made "the older girls laugh." But for the narrator
"it was unforeseen, but at the same time dreaded." Her
desire to keep her love pure of vulgarity intensified her desire not to know the reality from which he came: "it was

unbearable to think that his house might be slovenly and un-
painted. "

The young girl is headed for crisis. She retreats to
the beach where she can dream of the beauty of her love.
"I still would not care to say which was more real--the dream
I could make blossom at will, or the sight of the bathers. I
am presenting them, you see, only as simultaneous. " And
in their simultaneity, the worlds counterpoint each other.
They are exclusive and disintegrative. Her love is the "rose
forced into premature bloom. " The bathers on the beach are
"Common," "Lying in leglike confusion," "breasts hung heavy
and widening like pears. " The descriptions are sensual and
the sensual is ugly.

The narrator's vision of disgust increases. She is
horrified as one man pours sand between the woman's fat
breasts. Why juxtapose this incident with the vision of the
young boy at school? Her love for that boy has nothing in
common with the actions of these people. Yet, after the
man poured the sand down the fat woman's breasts, he "smiled,
the way panting dogs seem to be smiling, and gazed about
carelessly at them all and out over the water. He even looked
at me, and included me. Looking back, stunned, I wished
they were all dead. "

This knowledge of community is exactly what the young
girl wanted to protect herself from. This desire to retreat
into Platonism at those first prurient stirrings is the crisis
of young adolescence. "I tried to withdraw to my most inner
dream, that of touching the wrist of the boy I loved on the
stair; I felt a shudder of my wish shaking the darkness like
leaves where I had closed my eyes. .." The device of
framing was not necessarily to help gain knowledge of the
world, but to protect the girl from self-knowledge.

One might think this a story of artistic growth--the
narrator/artist dealing with the problems of her own involvement with humanity. Yet the narrator admits that "ever since
that day, I have been unable to bear the sight of blood. "
She speaks with a little too much sympathy for the young
girl who continued "to lie there, squaring my vision with my
hands. ... " She seems thankful for her ability to retreat
from the vulgarity and harshness she perceives in the real
world, feeling superior to those at its mercy.

I could even foresee the way he would stare back,

speechless and innocent, a medium-sized boy with blond hair, his unconscious eyes looking beyond me and out the window, solitary and unprotected.

Is this the "admirable objectivity" that Porter speaks of? It does allow for selectivity and for artistic control. But at the same time it creates a physical and mental gap that isolates the artist from his own community and thus his own humanity. The child is a psychological machine, far less sympathetic a character, finally, than the red-haired youth of "The Key."

However, if we compare "A Memory" with other stories in the collection, the blond-haired boy becomes one of a parade of overwhelmed blondes--Lily Daw, Albert Morgan, Ruby Fisher. Aren't these all characters the author seems to pity? How many stories end with the sense of the author pulling away from her characters, retreating as the young adolescent did, to the frame of her fingers? We see Bowman, his heart beating unheard in the dead of night, or old Mr. Marblehall living his own lonely fantasy, or the burnt-out lives of Jason and Sara Morton.

One might feel Welty suggesting that if the sensitive of the world are to survive, they must retreat somehow from its ugly and insulting aggressions. The portrait of the red-haired youth in "The Key" suggests the futility of felt moral responsibility. The paradox Welty presents then, is that the author must finally offer the world a detachment which is at once the source of creative vision and the source of his own personal failure.

The stories of A Curtain of Green are glorious in their style. But one feels a shrug of the artist's shoulders as she pulls away from her sorry cast of characters. They are not her concern. Her concern rather is one of artistic integrity, a search not uncommon to Welty's American predecessors: Hawthorne, Melville and James. Isolation is, finally, a personal damnation for all.

EUDORA WELTY'S THE ROBBER BRIDEGROOM
AND OLD SOUTHWEST HUMOR:
A Doubleness of Vision

by Charles E. Davis

     Eudora Welty's first novel, The Robber Bridegroom,
is one of her richest and most complex in terms of the va-
riety of themes it explores--the general history of a region,
the effects of the steady passage of time, the question of
personal identity, the inability to distinguish between reality
and fantasy, and the dual nature of both man and the world
he confronts. This complexity has been generally overlooked,
perhaps primarily because of the disarming and deceptively
simple method of Miss Welty's presentation. The style is
elemental, almost child-like, as she combines a number of
fairy tales from the Grimm brothers with Southern folk humor and legend. More important to the development of the
multiple themes, however, is the author's use of the tradition of the Old Southwest humorists.

     While one of the purposes of these humorists was
quite simply to provide comic entertainment for themselves
and for their audience, they were also attempting to capture
a short-lived period in the history of the southern United
States and its people--a period whose time and character
were rapidly passing out of existence. On the surface the
scenes and the individuals in their sketches are comic, often
hilarious; but while the reader laughs, he also feels the tremendous gap between his own time and that of an innocent,
fabulous world that, if indeed it ever existed, is forever lost
to him. It is this aspect of Southwest humor, this tension
between the comic and the serious, that Miss Welty so effectively utilizes in The Robber Bridegroom to develop her concept of the duality of all things--man, the wilderness, time,
history, and reality.

     The slightness of criticism concerning this work indi-

71

cates that it is the least understood of all Miss Welty's
novels. As late as 1968 Robert Daniel dismisses it by saying that "the fantasy called The Robber Bridegroom is only
for her [Miss Welty's] special admirers."[1] Without examining
the book in any detail, Ruth Vande Kieft, like many other
critics, finds that the author's "high spirits erupted fully in
The Robber Bridegroom."[2] Eunice Glenn moves toward suggesting the complexity of the book when she states that "The
tone is one of mock irony: you see the characters as ridiculous, while at the same time you are appalled at their evil."[3]
She goes on to say, "The convincing force of the story is in
the juxtaposition of the rough-and-tumble and grotesque life
in the wilderness with the conventional, the real ..." (p. 87).
But perhaps the most perceptive comment was made by Alfred
Kazin in a book review soon after the novel's publication in
1942:

> Here ... is what so many have been trying
> to capture by dint of will and bibliography alone--
> the lost fabulous innocence of our departed frontier....
> If this is an enchanted world, the black forest of
> childhood, it is also one into which the sadder,
> newer world is breaking. And the slow, long roll
> of disenchantment can be heard at the end ... as
> the axe that broke the trees only led the way for
> the machine that would break the forest.[4]

This assessment indicates the tension, so prevalent in the
Southwest humorists' sketches, by which Miss Welty develops
her theme of duality.

That Miss Welty is extremely conscious in this novel
of the Southwest humor tradition, there can be little doubt.
The list of subjects of frontier humor offered by Hennig
Cohen and William Dillingham in the introduction of their
Humor of the Old Southwest[5] is strikingly similar to the
following frontier pastimes enumerated in The Robber Bridegroom: "wrestling matches, horse races, gander pullings,
shooting matches, turkey shoots, or cockfights...."[6] Certainly the strong local color element in the tradition is captured in Miss Welty's description of the Old Natchez Trace,
the wilderness, and the outlaws and adventurers who inhab-
ited that world. The comic exaggerations and comic com-
parisons associated with the Southwest humorists also find
their way into the novel with amazing regularity. For example, we are told that the simple-minded boy Goat is so named
"because he could butt his way out the door when his mother

left him locked in, and equally, because he could butt his
way in when she left him locked out" (pp. 39-40). He is
described as having his "hair all matted up and the color
of carrots, and his two eyes so crossed they looked like
one. He smiled and he had every other tooth, but that was
all. He stood there with his two big toes sticking up" (p. 41).

Interesting though these examples may be, they merely
serve to indicate Miss Welty's utilization of Southwest humor
in this novel. The significance of that tradition for the reader
of The Robber Bridegroom lies in the humorist's essentially
dual vision of the frontier world, his blending of the humorous and the serious, his comic treatment of a now-vanished
era. The "lost fabulous innocence" that Kazin had spoken
of in 1942 finds its chief exemplar in the person of the fron-
tiersman-planter Clement Musgrove, "an innocent of the wilderness" (p. 182) who "had trusted the evil world" (p. 102).
That he realizes the time of innocence has passed is clearly
evident in his musing that "the time of cunning is of a world
I will have no part in" (p. 142). Even the delightful tall
tales of Clement's daughter Rosamond and of the riverboat-
man Mike Fink reinforce the reader's sense of separation
from this fabulous world. As Cohen and Dillingham put it,
"the effect of the tall tale comes from the reader's delighted
appreciation of the exaggerations and of the comic character
and his language in juxtaposition with the sad realization that
the events of the tale, the accomplishments of the protagonist,
could never really happen" (p. xx). Thus, Mike Fink's hyper-
bolic accounts of his own exploits amuse while simultaneously
removing irrevocably his gargantuan world from reality:

> I eat a whole cow at one time, and follow
> her up with a live sheep if it's Sunday. Ho! ho!
> If I get hungry on a voyage, I jump off my raft
> and wade across, and take whatever lies in my
> path on shore. When I come near, the good folk
> take to their heels, and run from their houses!
> I only laugh at the Indians, and I can carry a
> dozen oxen on my back at one time, and as for
> pigs, I tie them in a bunch and hang them from
> my belt (p. 9).

The dual nature of the Southwest humorist's attitude toward his material is heightened by a deliberately established
distance between himself and the world he is depicting. As
Walter Blair notes, recounted from a distance, "even the most
harrowing episode of a frontier tale might become comic."[7]

Looking at the sketches from the standpoint of a reader, Pascal Covici states that the total effect "is to insulate him [the reader] from any emotional involvement or identification with events, characters, or region."[8] Miss Welty, like the Southwest humorists, establishes a distance between herself and her story. Alun R. Jones describes her attitude toward her material as "detached, even ironic...."[9] Such an attitude allows Miss Welty to treat the horrors of murder, decapitation, torture, and rape--at least on the surface--as comic. The humorous depiction of death and decay and of cruelty and sadism, that is so much a part of the tradition of Southwest humor, is amply evident in The Robber Bridegroom. But despite the lighthearted treatment, death, after all, remains death; cruelty remains cruelty. The matter-of-fact recounting of Jamie Lockhart's rape of Rosamond Musgrove must not blind us to the fact that it is still a rape. Certainly, the disturbing reality of the following apparently off-hand remark made by Jamie concerning the Indians should be obvious to even the most casual of readers: "The savages are so clever they are liable to last out, no matter how we stamp upon them" [italics mine] (p. 21).

With both the relationship between the Southwest humor sketches and The Robber Bridegroom and the primary significance of that relationship established, the complexity of Miss Welty's vision of the frontier in this novel becomes more apparent. The doubleness of all things, the inextricable commingling of the pathos and the absurdity of life, allows man to see and comprehend very little either of himself or of the world. Neither Jamie Lockhart nor Mike Fink can effectively establish and maintain a single identity; Clement Musgrove is confounded by events that occur, apparently without his volition, in his own life; Rosamond Musgrove is forced to fantasize because the reality of her existence with her stepmother is intolerable; all the characters are helpless before the forces of time and change. As the detached narrator of these events, Miss Welty suggests through the entanglements of the personal lives of her characters the monumental task that confronts the twentieth-century mind that attempts to piece together and interpret the general history of a region.

The essential doubleness of all things most certainly includes man himself. Every man has, on the one hand, a private self--what Miss Welty calls a "who I am"--that he presents to the world. Only when he is in his proper time can he effectively unite these two selves. Mike Fink, for example, thinks of himself as a heroic part of the frontier, and as long as that frontier remains a reality, he insists upon his complete identity--insists, that is, upon both who and what he is. When he first meets Jamie Lockhart, he declares with relish that he is "none other than Mike Fink, champion of all the flatboat bullies on the Mississippi River...." (p. 8). Jamie's pretended refusal to believe him outrages Mike, who reacts with a violent threat: "Say once more that I am not Mike Fink and, peace or no peace, that will be your last breath!" (p. 12). Like Mike, the notorious outlaws, the Harp brothers, identify completely with the wilderness, and they insist at the end of every robbery upon calling out as they ride away, "We are the Harps!" (p. 155). As long as the frontier remains wild and free, people like Mike Fink and the Harps can follow their natural inclinations, but when the frontier begins to disappear, to become civilized, they are lost. The Harps, of course, die, their deaths corresponding to the closing of the frontier. But Mike lives, and unable to assimilate himself into the changing world, he becomes a man out of his time. When we last see him, he is, of all things, a mail rider, a position which places him as a link between person and person, between town and town, as a representative of civilization and communication. Unwilling to accept this new position forced upon him, he insists upon being "an anonymous mail rider" (p. 169). He tells Rosamond, "I won't say who I am" (p. 174) and sadly reflects that "in the old days" he was a "big ... figure in the world" (p. 175). Repeatedly pushed by Rosamond, Mike finally confesses, "Tell no one, but I am none other than Mike Fink! It would be outrageous if this were known, that the greatest flatboatman of them all came down in the world to be a mail rider on dry land. It would sound like the end of the world!" (p. 179). This ironic statement is, of course, nearer to the truth than Mike thinks. In good comic fashion Miss Welty assures us that Mike's "name was restored to its original glory" (p. 180), but the implication is, I think, that only in legend can he again be who and what he once was.

While Mike and the Harps immerse themselves totally in the life of the frontier, the bandit Jamie Lockhart feels a distance between himself and the wilderness. That is, his identity as a man must remain separate from his identity as a bandit. Early in the novel Jamie says to Clement, "Say who I am forever, but dare to say what I am, and that will be the last breath of any man" (p. 13). With this kind of rift between his public and private selves, Jamie does indeed lead a double life in the woods with his bride, Rosamond:

"The only thing that divided his life from hers was the raiding and the robbing he did, but that was like his other life, that she could not see, and so she contented herself with loving all that was visible and present of him as much as she was able" (pp. 85-86). Not until his total identity is threatened with extinction does Jamie cry, late in the novel, "Not a man in the world can say I am not who I am and what I am, and live!" (p. 157). Despite this statement, however, Jamie continues to feel that his place is not in the frontier world. This fact is most obvious when he is given the opportunity to divorce himself completely from his old life as a bandit. The severed head of the outlaw Big Harp has been incorrectly identified as that of Jamie Lockhart. Having therefore lost his old identity, Jamie can incorporate himself with impunity into the new civilized world of the city and become known as Jamie Lockhart, merchant.

Just as the men of the wilderness have this dual nature, so also does the wilderness itself, at one moment being peaceful and gentle and at the next, savage and foreboding. When Jamie and Rosamond share one of their rare quiet days together, the forest seems an idyllic spot:

> One day Jamie did not ride away with the others, and then the day was night and the woods were the roof over their heads. The tender flames of the myrtle trees and green smoke of the cedars were the fires of their hearth. In the radiant noon they found the shade, and ate the grapes from the muscadine vines. The spice-dreams floated through their heads when they stretched their limbs and slept in the woods. The stream lay still in the golden ravine, the water glowing darkly, the colors of fruits and nuts (p. 86).

But this is only one of the faces that the wilderness shows, for it is also a place of danger and death. As Rosamond, for example, walks through the forest on one of the perilous errands devised by her stepmother, she comes to a deep and dark ravine. "And at the foot of the ravine ran the Old Natchez Trace, that old buffalo trail where travelers passed along and were set upon by the bandits and the Indians and torn apart by the wild animals" (pp. 43-44). Is the wilderness a garden generously providing man his basic needs, or is it a dark and evil place where the unwary will be swallowed up? This is the question that plagues Clement as he muses over the nature of man and the world:

What is the place and time? Here are all
possible trees in a forest, and they grow as tall
and as great and as close to one another as they
could ever grow in the world. Upon each limb is
a singing bird and across this floor, slowly and
softly and forever moving into profile, is always
a beast, one of a procession, weighted low with
his burning coat, looking from the yellow eye set
in its head (p. 141).

Clement's reflection about time and place sounds what
is perhaps the most persistent theme in the book--the relationship between the past, the present, and the future.
Man's identity is tied inextricably to his attitudes both toward
the past and toward the future. For Clement his old life before the death of his first wife, Amalie, at the hands of the
Indians is infinitely more desirable than his present life with
his second wife, Salome. But the past is forever closed to
him except in his dreams. In those dreams, he tells Jamie,
"whenever I lie down, then it is the past. When I climb to
my feet, then it is the present. And I keep up a struggle
not to fall" (p. 29). For an individual like Clement, then,
the distinction between reality and fantasy is difficult, even
undesirable, to ascertain. As for Mike Fink, the riverboat-
man turned mail rider, he yearns for the world of "the old
days" when he was a "big figure in the world" (p. 175).
When Rosamond, who is much more concerned with the future
than the past, tells him she has a message for Jamie "from
another world"--that of the future--Mike immediately assumes
it to be "a message from out of the past...." (p. 177). Both
Rosamond's use of the phrase "from another world" and Mike's
erroneous assumption point out poignantly the enormity of the
gap between the way of life associated with the past and that
offered by the future. Before his change from bandit to merchant Jamie thinks he has "it all divisioned off into time and
place, and that many things were for later and for further
away...." (p. 87). But in the world of The Robber Bridegroom life is not so neat and man does not so easily control
his own destiny. Only after his acceptance of the future offered by Rosamond, only after his acceptance of the new
world and his place in it can Jamie have "the power to look
both ways and to see a thing from all sides" (p. 185). For
some, then, the passage of time brings a new and better
world. For others the future brings only a world into which
they cannot assimilate themselves. They are forced by time
and circumstance, by what Clement calls "a great tug at the
whole world ..." (p. 21) into changes with which hearts and

wills may have had nothing to do. Unable to reconstruct the past, they become anachronisms, reliving through dreams or recalling in legend old times forever gone.

As has already been stated, the old Southwest humorists had been concerned with chronicling the life of a frontier period that even in its heyday was in a state of rapid transition. Maintaining a detached attitude, they could present this world, despite the flux that characterized it, essentially as a comic one. Adopting the same disinterested stance, Miss Welty, too, depicts the history of a frontier continually undergoing change. With the coming of the white settlers the Indians somehow intuitively realize that the end of their way of life is imminent: "'The Indians know their time has come,' said Clement. 'They are sure of the future growing smaller always....'" (p. 21). The history of the white man's intrusion into this world is traced by Clement as he recounts to Jamie the details of his own personal history. Clement reconstructs his movement from the settled and peaceful hills of Virginia southwestward to the Natchez Trace when he was somehow caught up seemingly against his will by the heady spirit of adventure and expansion. His transition from pioneer to planter, his change from wanderer and explorer to owner and tiller of the land, is equally puzzling to him. The cost of his move from Virginia has been great: the loss of his first wife, his son, his friends, and his happiness. The shrewish Salome insists that he own more and more land, clear more and more of the forest, and build bigger and better houses. Her attitude toward the land obviously parallels that of the rapacious plantation owners who came to ravage the wilderness:

> "Next year," said Salome, and she shaded
> her eagle eye with her eagle claw, and scanned
> the lands from east to west, "we must cut down
> more of the forest, and stretch away the fields
> until we grow twice as much of everything. Twice
> as much indigo, twice as much cotton, twice as
> much tobacco. For the land is there for the taking,
> and I say, if it can be taken, take it" (p. 99).

Clement believes, however, that man's attempts to carve from the wilderness such large monuments to himself are futile, that permanence is merely illusory: "The savages have only come the sooner to their end; we will come to ours too. Why have I built my house and added to it? The planter will go after the hunter, and the merchant after the

planter, all having their day" (p. 161). Jamie also acknowledges the transition, for he knows that "the bandit's life is
done with...." (p. 166). His metamorphosis from outlaw to
respectable merchant is perhaps most clearly exemplified by
the religious ceremony complete with priest when he marries
Rosamond, presumably for a second time. Fulfilling Clement's prophecy that the merchant will come after the planter,
Jamie settles with Rosamond into a routine and reputable life
in New Orleans.

Because of the fairy-tale atmosphere maintained by
Miss Welty throughout this book, one might be tempted to
assume that the young couple will live happily ever after.
But the general tenor of the novel will not allow such an
interpretation without considerable qualification. The sug-
gestion of doubleness, the blending of the comic and the serious which is prevalent in so many of the Southwest humorists'
sketches in general and in The Robber Bridegroom in particular, depends in part upon the reader's realization that the
characters and deeds depicted are so short-lived, so subject
to the passage of time. If the times of the hunter and planter
pass rapidly, there is little reason to believe that the time
of the merchant will be substantially different. Few passages
in this book suggest permanence. There are, however, two
quite tenuous exceptions. One of Clement's reflections on
the passage of time ironically reveals, by implication only,
a kind of permanence (not unlike that found in the poetry of
Wallace Stevens) in the changing of the seasons:

> Spring and the clear and separate leaves
> mounting to the top of the sky, the black flames of
> cedars, the young trees shining like the lanterns,
> the magnolias softly ignited; Summer and the vines
> falling down over the darkest caves, red and green,
> changing to the purple of grapes and the Autumn
> descending in a golden curtain; then in the naked-
> ness of the Winter wood the buffalo on his sinking
> trail, pawing the ice till his forlock hangs in the
> spring, and the deer following behind to the salty
> places to transfix his tender head. And that was
> the way the years went by (pp. 141-142).

A more explicit example is the Indians' unshakable belief in
a timeless realm beyond the clouds. When the redoubtable
Salome commands the sun to stand still, the Indian chief
tells her, "One like you cannot force him, for his home is
above the clouds, in a tranquil place. He is the source of

our tribe and of everything, and therefore he does not and will not stand still, but continues forever" (p. 163). Yet even these two instances indicate, at least in this world, that time inexorable passes, that it cannot be commanded to "stand still."

Careful examination of the novel and the major tradition which lies behind it makes it difficult to understand those who see in it mainly an exuberation of Miss Welty's spirits and a fairy-tale celebration of the history of her region. These elements are certainly there. But humor, as we all know, is a vehicle through which the pathos, even the tragedy of human experience can be revealed. The humorists of the old Southwest, writing primarily between 1835 and 1860, captured both the comedy and the pathos of an era that, even as they observed it, was quickly passing away. Miss Welty, approximately a century further removed from that era, has, like those humorists before her, traced with both a loving and an ironic hand the essential doubleness of the life and times of her subjects, has depicted that blend of the comic and the serious that is human existence. The result, I think, is one of her most rewarding and significant works.

Notes

[1] "The World of Eudora Welty," in Southern Renascence, ed. Louis Rubin and Robert Jacobs (Baltimore: The Johns Hopkins Press, 1968), p. 307.

[2] Eudora Welty (New York: Twayne Publishers, Inc., 1962), p. 165.

[3] "Fantasy in the Fiction of Eudora Welty," in A Southern Vanguard, ed. Allen Tate (New York: Prentice-Hall, Inc., 1947), p. 85.

[4] "An Enchanted World in America," New York Herald Tribune Book Review, vol. 19, no. 9 (25 October 1942), p. 19.

[5] (Boston: Houghton Mifflin Company, 1964) p. xiii.

[6] Eudora Welty, The Robber Bridegroom (Garden City: Doubleday, Doran and Company, Inc., 1942), p. 40. This and all subsequent quotations from The Robber Bridegroom

are taken from this edition and will be cited by page number within the text.

[7]Native American Humor (New York: American Book Company, 1937), p. 92.

[8]Mark Twain's Humor: The Image of a World (Dallas: Southern Methodist Univ. Press, 1962), p. 6.

[9]"The World of Love: The Fiction of Eudora Welty," in The Creative Present: Notes on Contemporary American Fiction, ed. Nona Balakian and Charles Simmons (Garden City: Doubleday and Company, Inc., 1963), p. 184.

METRONOME AND MUSIC: THE ENCOUNTER
BETWEEN HISTORY AND MYTH
IN THE GOLDEN APPLES

by Douglas Messerli

Although according to Eudora Welty, The Golden
Apples (1949) is a book of short stories, nevertheless, as
Thomas L. McHaney has recently noted, "it ... manages
to create a complex unified impression in the manner of the
novel."[1] Certainly, an appreciation of the structural and
thematic density of the whole is lost if the work is considered merely in its parts. As McHaney has shown, the book
as a whole functions almost as a musical composition, structured according to various and diverse mythological analogues.
To a lesser degree, several other critics have also explored
some of these mythological patterns,[2] but thus far no one
except McHaney has recognized the vast importance of these
analogues to the structure and the philosophical matter of
the work, and even McHaney has failed to note that Welty's
concern with myth, as sweeping as it is, is but half of her
conception in The Golden Apples. For this book is also
deeply grounded in Welty's concept of time, and here specifically she considers not merely the problem of time, but
the order of time. Knowing that time may be seen as occur-
ring either in a linear or a cyclical pattern, that time may
be experienced either as history[3] or as myth, Welty has
structured the individual stories and, consequently, the whole
book around the encounter between these two perceptions of
the order of time.

On one hand, The Golden Apples is a history. It is
a series of stories ordered chronologically which concern the
small Mississippi town of Morgana from a period before World
War I until post-World War II, a span of about forty years.[4]
Within this time-span Welty's characters move in linear time;
they are born, they mature, and some of them die. Indeed,
a great part of the power of the work as a whole derives

from this historical framework. As one watches characters
such as the MacLain twins, Cassie Morrison, Virgie Rainey,
Nina Carmichael and Jinny Love Stark grow from childhood
to maturity, one cannot but come to love and judge them, to
feel linked to them in the same way they and the townspeople
do to one another. In Morgana, as in any small town, because of this shared experience in linear time, the individual's life is inextricably connected with, is even defined by,
the lives of the others in the community. But this fact can
also bring about a destructive set of circumstances in which
individual lives become community property and individual
acts lose meaning or, because they are seen as a threat to
the homogeneity of the community, are outrightly opposed.

Welty establishes this idea immediately in "Shower of
Gold" by having the narrative carried by Katie Rainey, who,
friendly, somewhat wise and neighborly gossip that she is,
chooses to tell the reader, not her own story, but the story
of King MacLain. It is a history which Katie imparts to the
reader, the history of a man who, free from traditional
morality, leaves his wife Snowdie only to return for a few
hours every so many years to impregnate her as he has half
the women in the countryside. But it is a history in which
Katie and the whole community unwillingly partake,[5] for,
obviously, such behavior is a threat to community values.
As Katie reports early in her narrative concerning King's
comings and goings, "We might have had a little run on doing
that in Morgana, if it had been so willed."[6] It has not been
"so willed," Katie implies, because she and her fellow townspeople have selected and reordered the events as they occur-
red. Katie's story concentrates not upon King MacLain's individual exploits, but upon the community conspiracy to keep
from Snowdie the truth about King's penultimate attempt to
return home, when his twin sons, dressed in masks for Halloween and wearing roller skates, unknowingly scared off
their father. Although this story is hilariously comic, there
are quite serious implications to it, for, as the story belies,
Katie and the community have attempted to control the lives
of those around them by converting individual action into history, a history which like all histories is created by the historian taking events in linear time and reinterpreting them
according to his vision of reality. Katie may feel slightly
guilty for the reinterpretation--Katie suggests that Snowdie
"kind of holds it against me, because I was there that day
when he come ..." (p. 18)--but she believes that it is necessary in order to protect the community from the outside,
from a world of threatening and chaotic modes of existence.

Indeed, even in telling her history, in her pretense of confidentiality, Katie attempts to draw the reader into the community; despite protestations that she tells her tale to the reader only because he is a "passerby, that will never see her [Snowdie] again, or me either" (p. 3), Katie invites, almost insists through sharing the reality behind her history, that he partake of the community sensibility.

On the other hand, in "Shower of Gold" one recognizes a pattern, directly opposed to history, of which it is clear that Katie has little awareness. For Katie's narrative implies far more than she comprehends. She fears that Snowdie blames her for being there the day of King's return, but it is doubtful that she believes that Snowdie has any reason to blame her. While Katie sees that there is something special about King MacLain--as she says, "With men like King, your thoughts are bottomless" (p. 17)--she lacks the vision to see King in the proper perspective. In her historical view of reality she can only see King as a threat, as a special type of man, a "man with manners," of whom she cautions the reader to beware (p. 4). Fate, her own husband, the type of man she prefers, "is more down to earth" (p. 17). It is only in their literalness that events and people have meaning to her. When she asks her husband to describe what King looked like while riding in the inauguration parade with Governor Vardaman, where Fate claims he spotted King, she takes a broom to her husband for imitating "a horse and man in one" (p. 9). She has not the gift, the imagination to perceive that King has mythological qualities, that he may indeed be a centaur. And like many visionless people, she insists that it is others, not she, who cannot see. Snowdie, according to Katie, is a "blinky"-eyed albino who has never "ever got a good look at life, maybe. Maybe from the beginning. Maybe she just doesn't know the extent. Not the kind of look I got, and away back when I was twelve year old or so. Like something was put to my eye" (p. 7). Again, when she hears of people claiming to see King in New Orleans and Mobile at the same time, Katie responds, "That's people's careless ways of using their eyes" (p. 10).

Katie understands nothing that occurs simultaneously. From her historical perspective, "time goes like a dream no matter how hard you run, and all the time we heard things from out in the world that we listened to but that still didn't mean we believed them" (p. 9). She admits, in other words, that reality for her is like a dream, with several layers of meaning; but it is an enemy for that very reason, because

she cannot make sense of it. She attempts, therefore, to
outrun time, to make it into the past so that she can take
away its dream-like quality and grasp it. But time always
wins and confuses life. Thus, Katie suggests, things outside
of her narrow purview of experienced history cannot be believed. Reality exists only in the community, for the community is close at hand, and, as I have implied, it creates
history. The community unifies, regulates and equalizes
reality, and, in so doing, ends confusion, destroys simultaneity. Accordingly, after Snowdie meets King on the bank
of the river and returns pregnant, looking as if "a shower
of something had struck her" (p. 6), Katie fears for her.
For even if Katie cannot recognize what has happened to
Snowdie, she does perceive that, struck with that "shower
of something," Snowdie is set apart. Thus, to keep Snowdie
from being "by her own self," "Everybody tried to stay with
her as much as they could spare, not let a day go by without one of us to run in and speak to her and say a word
about an ordinary thing" (p. 8). But, of course, it is no
"ordinary thing" that has happened to Snowdie. As Ruth Vande
Kieft has pointed out, like Danaë, Snowdie has been impreg-
nated by Zeus (King) in a "shower of gold."[7] Thus, when
years later on that day when King tries and fails to return,
in trying to protect her, in "fabricating," Katie and her
friends cheat Snowdie out of partaking once more of another
reality. As with Danaë, who was kept locked in a subterranean chamber, they keep Snowdie in their subterranean
chamber of community where time exists merely as the past.

    In "June Recital" Cassie Morrison replaces Katie
Rainey as historian. Like Katie, she tells a story from
memory. Tie-dying a scarf in her room one summer after-
noon, Cassie is made to remember by hearing a phrase of
music. The phrase, from the recital piece entitled Für
Elise, recalls for her a scrap of language which, in turn,
brings forth memories of her childhood piano lessons with
Miss Eckhart, who had then rented out the bottom floor of
the now-decaying MacLain house next door. Zelma Turner
Howard, in her chapter on time in The Rhetoric of Eudora
Welty's Short Stories, has suggested that Welty is here using
time in the Proustian sense, and indeed, there are similar-
ities.[8] But, once again, it is not a personal history that
Cassie recalls as much as it is a community one. For,
several of Morgana's children, including Jinny Love Stark,
Parnell Moody, Missie Spights, the MacLain twins and, most
importantly, Katie Rainey's daughter Virgie, also take lessons
from Miss Eckhart, and it is their stories more than her own
that Cassie relates.

The history of Miss Eckhart and her pupils is one of frustration and despair. Miss Eckhart, having come to Morgana for what reason no one knows, has spent her energy and accomplishment on the unpromising pupils such as Cassie, with only Virgie Rainey showing any particular talent. Thus, Cassie remembers the phrase, "Virgie Rainey, danke schoen," Miss Eckhart's continual sign of recognition and praise of her favorite, whom Miss Eckhart insists must "go out into the world," away from Morgana to be "heard from" (p. 53). To the rest of her students Miss Eckhart reveals little evidence of any feeling save an unvarying strictness and a hatred of flies. As Cassie and her friends play, their teacher sits with flyswatter in hand, ready to come down upon their wrists if a fly should alight, otherwise entirely motionless and silent except for an occasional leaning forward to write on the child's music the word "slow" or "practice." The only other essential of Miss Eckhart's lessons is the presence of her metronome. As Cassie observes, "Miss Eckhart worshiped her metronome" (p. 40). It is that adoration which, among other things, makes Cassie and her friends suspect that there are other aspects of Miss Eckhart's personality. Virgie, who seems to be oblivious to Miss Eckhart's praise and love, one day refuses to continue to play another note if the metronome is not taken away, and thereafter, Virgie is made an exception to Miss Eckhart's metronome requirement. It is this event, and Virgie's general disrespect for Miss Eckhart that enlightens Cassie concerning "changes" in her piano teacher:

> Anybody could tell that Virgie was doing something to Miss Eckhart. She was turning her from a teacher into something lesser. And if she was not a teacher, what was Miss Eckhart?
> There were times when Miss Eckhart's Yankeeness, if not her very origin, some last quality to fade, almost faded. Before some caprice of Virgie's, her spirit drooped its head. The child had it by the lead. Cassie saw Miss Eckhart's spirit as a terrifyingly gentle water-buffalo cow in the story of "Peasie and Beansie" in the reader. And sooner or later, after taming her teacher, Virgie was going to mistreat her. Most of them expected some great scene (pp. 41-42).

Indeed, a "great scene" does soon occur, although it is not one that any of them have foreseen. On a rainy day when Cassie, Virgie and Jinny stay after their lessons in Miss Eckhart's studio-apartment to wait for a downpour to let up, Miss Eckhart plays a sonata which, Cassie reports, if it "had an origin in a place on earth, it was a place where Virgie, even, had never been and was not likely ever to go" (p. 49). The listening children, hardly daring to move, are made "uneasy, almost alarmed" by the performance, which they see as if "something had burst out, unwanted, exciting from the wrong person's life" (pp. 49-50). Later, when the local shoe salesman drowns--a man named Mr. Sissum whom the children recognize that Miss Eckhart is "sweet on"--the community is presented with another "great scene" in which Miss Eckhart breaks "out of the circle" of mourners at the burial and is caught before going "headlong into the red clay hole" (p. 47). It is because of this demonstration of grief that the Morgana mothers begin to stop their children from taking lessons. Finally, some time after, Virgie's stopping lessons takes away "Miss Eckhart's luck for good" (p. 56), and she goes "down out of sight" (p. 58).

Cassie, like Katie Rainey, is unaware of what her history implies. She does not recognize in her memories of Miss Eckhart that she has witnessed a woman torn between a linear and a cyclical view of time. Cassie's view of time is, like Katie's, historical and linear, and, thus, she cannot comprehend her teacher's struggle. Cassie has never been able to play the piano without the metronome. It is only Virgie who can reject the bullying order of the metronome with its incessant reminder of time perpetually moving forward; it is only Virgie who can draw her teacher away from that narrow view of time which has come to rule Miss Eckhart's frustrated existence. Virgie is special. What Welty shows the reader through Cassie's memories is that with Virgie's help, Miss Eckhart begins to loose herself from the exacting demands of historical time, that through the creative imagination, which among her students Virgie alone is sensitive of, Miss Eckhart comes to terms with a different kind of time, the kind of time of which Cassie had a glimpse when Miss Eckhart played for them on that rainy day, the kind of time which, like the music itself, is new and old at the same moment, like all music made new each time it is repeated. It is the time of myth.

Cassie's failure to perceive this is at the heart of Miss Eckhart's frustration. In her historicism Cassie represents the community, for, as I have hinted, history in The Golden Apples is always communal, is always a social phenomenon. Thus, the community and Cassie's awarenesses are one and the same, a fact of which Miss Eckhart seems

to be cognizant from the start. One may conjecture that
Miss Eckhart's insistence that Virgie leave Morgana is an
expression of new possibility for what she herself has attempted and failed. For, it is implied by her origin that
Miss Eckhart was once a wanderer like King MacLain. One
suspects, however, that Miss Eckhart has stumbled into a
cage of sorts, where in order to survive she has imposed
upon herself the strict order of the metronome. Moreover,
it may be that in a world of historicism the use of the metronome is the only way to teach a concept of time. Miss Eckhart's flyswatter attacks on the wrists of her pupils is perhaps a subtle way of punishing them for their failure to grasp
the idea of that other kind of time. Certainly, Miss Eckhart
has been sensitive to myth all along. As McHaney points
out, Miss Eckhart's recitals are clearly a rite of spring,
and throughout The Golden Apples she is associated with
mythological figures such as Circe, Eurydice, Perseus and
others. It appears that Virgie serves primarily as a catalyst
for freeing Miss Eckhart once again from linear order, for
opening her to the life of the wanderer. But Miss Eckhart
is too old to wander and, staying in Morgana, she is recognized as an individual opposed to communal history; her actions are interpreted to be a threat to social order. [9] Cassie's
suspicions concerning Miss Eckhart's disintegration prove
correct. In the society where she remains, breaking "out
of the circle" can only bring destruction upon her.

In "June Recital," then, Welty has, as in "Shower of
Gold," brought together two sets of seemingly opposing forces:
history and myth, community and the individual. But here
she reexpresses these oppositions in the very structure of
the story. While Cassie sits in her room and recalls the
past, her brother Loch, in bed with malarial fever, observes
the events of the present in the run-down MacLain house next
door. Given his father's telescope because he is ill, Loch
is able to watch the comings and goings of several people,
including Virgie Rainey, who with her usual precocity has a
sailor in hand. They romp in the room upstairs while, unknown to them, Miss Eckhart, having walked into town from
the old people's home, enters below and there, after stuffing
the room with torn newspaper, and setting out her once-pre-
cious metronome, she tries to burn down the house and acci-
dentally sets fire to herself. Old Man Moody, the town mar-
shal, and Mr. Fatty Bowles also happen by (they have come
to awaken Mr. Holifield, the nightwatchman, who has been
sleeping in the house through the whole affair) and, after a
farcical series of attempts, eventually put out the house fire

and the fire in Miss Eckhart's hair, and take her away to
the mental asylum, while the final caller on the old MacLain
house, King MacLain, home again from his wanderings, looks
on. In other words, it has been Miss Eckhart herself playing
the phrase of music which triggered Cassie's memory. Thus,
Welty ironically demonstrates once more that Cassie has only
memory, that she can only participate in history. Unlike
Loch, she is unable to look upon the present which has con-
nections with all of the past and future time. Loch calls to
her from his room to come join him, but Cassie's answer
is telling, "I ain't got time." In fact, Cassie does not have
a sense of time other than her historicism. She does not
have the capability to look upon the multitudinous reality of
the present.

Loch has that capability. Because he does not know
as much of the past, he misinterprets the events which he
witnesses; he is a poor historian. Nevertheless, he employs
what he does know of the past to make sense of the present.
The rest he fills in with imagination. And, with these two,
with history and imagination (which is at the heart of myth),
Loch discovers a meaning which transcends the literal reality.
As with the music of Miss Eckhart, he gives an order to the
world in his especial and personal vision which is both old
and new. To Loch, Miss Eckhart is logically the "sailor's
mother" come to the house after her son who is upstairs,
and, as she rips newspaper, he comes to believe that she
is decorating the room as if for a party. Gradually, however, he perceives that, in the "splendor" with which the old
woman continues to decorate long after everything seems "fan-
ciful and beautiful enough," she is "all alone," that she is
"not connected with anything else, with anybody. She was
one old woman in the house not bent on dealing punishment"
(pp. 27-28). Loch comes to understand that the old woman
intends to burn down the house. At first he is vexed, not
so much because of the loss of the house which he has come
to claim for his own, but because she is going about setting
the place on fire the wrong way: she leaves the windows
shut tight, allowing for no draft. But when she takes out
the metronome and sets it on the piano, Loch is newly fas-
cinated by her slow, bird-like movements, for he now pre-
sumes that the box contains dynamite which will be set off
by the fire in the piano. Old Man Moody and Mr. Fatty
Bowles, men whom Loch recognizes, arrive just in time to
put out the fire, but the other man who happens along and
watches Moody and Bowles' antics through a window as if it
were a show, Loch mistakenly identifies. Having no remem-

brance of King MacLain, Loch thinks he is Mr. Voight, an
ex-roomer at the MacLain house in the days of the piano
lessons, who had promised Loch a talking bird that could say
"Rabbits. " Meanwhile, the two men inside discover the ticking metronome, and coming to the same conclusion as Loch,
Fatty Bowles throws it out the window. The metronome falls
into the weeds just below where Loch has crawled out onto a
tree, and Loch retrieves the object. After examining it, he
touches and stops its pendulum, takes away its key, poles
the stick into the box and secrets it away as if it were a
prize.

What is noteworthy here is that, through his fevered
imagination, Loch has made several conclusions which are
closer to "reality" than is Cassie's history. Loch immediately makes a connection between the actions of the couple upstairs and those of the woman below, but he also makes the perception that, despite that connection, Miss Eckhart is terribly
alone and separated from that couple. Loch's first belief,
that Miss Eckhart is decorating the room as if for a party,
is also not far from the truth, for Miss Eckhart's prepara-
tions for and setting fire to the house is like a party; it is
ritualistic. It is evident that in burning the house Miss Eckhart is attempting, in the mythological sense, to stop the
flux of time, the time of history, and, with the destruction
of what is left of the old, with the destruction of that history,
to permit a rejuvenation, a beginning anew. [10] Moreover,
Loch's association of King MacLain with the man who had
promised Loch a bird that could say "Rabbits" is not far
from correct, for, as McHaney points out, King MacLain
is associated throughout The Golden Apples with rabbits, [11]
a fact which will become more evident in the story entitled
"Sir Rabbit. " Finally, and most importantly, Loch recognizes the destructive potentiality of the metronome, of time
as seen merely in linear motion, and just as Virgie has previously been able to free herself from that time, so is Loch
able to control it; he stops the metronome. As he sits in
the sandpile with his new possession buttoned under his shirt,
momentarily freed from that destructive rush of time, Loch
hears "nothing ticking" but the repetitive music of the crick-
ets--who keep the time of nature and myth--and the sound of
"the train going through, ticking its two cars over the Big
Black Bridge" (p. 77)--which suggests that in the future, in
linear time, Loch will leave Morgana to become one of the
special people, a wanderer, who partakes of myth. [12]

That evening, Cassie, having returned home from a

community hay ride, lies thinking in her bed. She recognizes that Miss Eckhart and Virgie Rainey are "human beings terribly at large, roaming on the face of the earth. And there were others of them--human beings, roaming like lost beasts" (p. 85), but Cassie also understands that she is unlike them. As Welty writes of Cassie earlier in the book:

> She could not see herself do an unknown thing. She was not Loch, she was not Virgie Rainey; she was not her mother. She was Cassie in her room, seeing the knowledge and torment beyond her reach, standing at her window singing--in a voice soft, rather full today, and halfway thinking it was pretty (p. 68).

Even as she has a glimpse once again of that other kind of being and time, even as she recalls Yeats' "The Song of the Wandering Aengus" (the poem central to The Golden Apples because it concerns the search for fulfillment through wandering and myth), even as the lines of the poem run perfectly through Cassie's head, the lines vanish as they go, the reader is told, "one line yielding to the next, like a torch race" (p. 85), exactly as life itself vanishes in the linear and historical view of time. In the middle of the night Cassie sits up in her bed and repeats out loud one of the lines, "Because a fire was in my head;" but no fire is in her head. The fire has been in Loch, sick with malarial fever, and in Miss Eckhart whose hair caught fire. Cassie falls back, "unresisting." The face that was in the poem looks in only in her dreams, and, like Katie, Cassie cannot make sense of a reality which exists as dream.

From two different windows then, Welty has made clear that there are two perspectives of time, and she continues to work with these perspectives throughout the rest of the book. The next story, "Sir Rabbit," perfectly counterpoints "Shower of Gold," for in "Sir Rabbit" the two events which occur years apart are narrated not through the voice of a historian, but are seen rather through the eyes of Mattie Will as she is raped first by the MacLain twins, and later by King MacLain himself. Mattie is not only one who, like Snowdie, directly partakes of myth, but she is one who has heard the myth told and believed it from the start. "Oh-oh. I know you, Mr. King MacLain!" she cries, "I know the way you do" (p. 86). But it is not King this first time; it is his twin sons, who are the "spitting image" of King. And, although they may be somewhat lesser than King, Zeus him-

self, although she sees them as two "little meanies coming
now that she'd never dreamed of, instead of the one that
would have terrified her for the rest of her days" (p. 87),
Mattie, nevertheless, obliges and, thus, partakes of myth.
As she waits for the two boys to come at her, Mattie feels
"at that moment as though somewhere a little boat was going
out on a lake, never to come back" (p. 87). In other words,
like all experiences grounded in myth, the rape makes Mattie
feel as if something is beginning anew, from the beginning.
The sex act itself takes her back to the beginning, to the
original knowledge, to the time just before the fall.[13] Thus,
again, in Mattie's surrender one can see, just as in Miss
Eckhart's music, the old is made new. Even the twins' actions are ritualistic: They first make a "tinkling" circle
around her, rape her, and then sit in a circle eating many
sticks of candy until a crow calls over their heads; then,
they all get to their feet "as though a clock struck" (p. 88)
and, together, they say "Now" and walk away from her back-
wards before running off. It is as if time has been momentarily overcome before the present begins again with the
spoken "now"; it is the very essence of myth.

When she is threatened by King years after, Mattie
is even more willing to participate in myth, to become
"something she had always heard of" (p. 95). Through King
she recognizes that she will be made something other than
herself, that she will become "Mr. MacLain's Doom, or
Mr. MacLain's Weakness," and being what he has left her,
she will thus fulfill the patrimony of her maiden name, Sojourner; for, although she stays behind, married to Junior
Holifield, she will always be a wanderer at heart. The after-
math of this rape is actually expressed in music, in what I
have been suggesting is the perfect analogy of myth. Mattie
sings a song which is concerned with that magical and mysterious world of which she has just partaken:

> In the night time,
> At the right time
> So I've understood
> 'Tis the habit of Sir Rabbit
> To dance in the wood--(p. 97).

But, as Ruth Vande Kieft has suggested, there is something
deprecating about the rhyme.[14] Something has happened to
the myth. King has grown older, and Mattie is aware that
in his "affront of body" and "sense" there is something "frantic" about his existence. After sex King falls asleep, and is

horrified to awaken and find Mattie watching him. And horrified he might well be, for during his sleep she has seen
his body in parts "looking no more driven than her man's
now, or of any more use than a heap of cane thrown up by
the mill and left in the pit to dry" (pp. 96-97). For Mattie
the myth has begun to disintegrate, perhaps because she has
looked at it too carefully, perhaps because it has been fragmented. Mattie now looks upon the earlier experience with
the twins almost with nostalgia. "For the first time," the
reader is told, "Mattie Will thought they [the twins] were
mysterious and sweet--gamboling now she knew not where"
(p. 98). That previous participation in myth is for Mattie
more meaningful than communion with the myth of which she
has heard all her life. And, with that new look to the past,
one perceives the beginnings of the transformation of myth
to historicism. Perhaps Mattie has changed, or perhaps the
times have.

In either case, it is clear in "Moon Lake" that the
world has become more complex. The societal urge which
ruled Katie in "Shower of Gold" is more developed in this
story, and the communal pressure is stronger, more ensnaring.
All of this is made ironic because the action of "Moon Lake"
takes place at a supposed retreat from society, a girls' summer camp. Jinny Love Stark, grown older,[15] and Nina Carmichael are definitely the representatives of this social order, and the orphans, led by a girl named Easter, and the
blacks who work at the camp are clearly outcasts. The only
person free from this dichotomous structure is Loch Morrison,
now a Boy Scout and Life Saver, who has pitched a tent some
distance from everyone else. Accordingly, Welty has set the
stage for another encounter between history and myth. But
this time the encounter is made more complicated through
its occurrence in a world that is very self-aware. Previously, both Katie and Cassie could not always recognize differences between themselves and those with the ability to
partake of myth; and to those in whom they did recognize
that special awareness, they were protective or, at most,
insistent in their attempts to draw them closer to the communal circle and the historical sensibility. But in this new
age, Jinny and Nina, completely aware of distinctions, either
reject the differences outright or try to possess them.

As Welty presents her, Jinny Live Stark is completely
conscious of her role as societal spokesman. For example,
Jinny suggests to the camp councilor, Mr. Gruenwald, in
"the cheerful voice she adopted toward grown people":

> Let's let the orphans go in the water first and get
> the snakes stirred up ... Then they'll be chased
> away by the time we go in (p. 101).

At another time when Easter suggests that Jinny, Nina and
she play "mumblety-peg," a game neither of the Morgana
girls knows how to play, Jinny asks, while "closing the
circle": "Who would even want to know?" This "not wanting to know" is precisely Jinny's stance. For the society
she represents no longer claims to have special vision; theirs
is the only vision. Jinny knowingly rejects all realities save
her own.

Nina, on the other hand, wants terribly to partake of
those realities; she wants more than anything to possess the
talents she sees in Easter. Indeed, the compulsion to possess seems the best way to describe the force which rules
Nina. Just as she possesses her drinking cup which she
permits no one to share, and of which Jinny says, "You don't
know Nina ... You'd think it was made of fourteen-carat gold,
and didn't come out of the pocket of an old suitcase, that
cup" (p. 107), so must Nina possess Easter's ability to share
in nature and myth, the capability which Nina sees in Easter's
open hand as she sleeps, to be one with the night:

> Easter's hand hung down, opened outward. Come
> here, night, Easter might say, tender to a giant,
> to such a dark thing. And the night, obedient and
> graceful, would kneel to her. Easter's calloused
> hand hung open there to the night that had got
> wholly into the tent (p. 123).

Pitiably, Nina opens her hand, stretches it and tries intellec-
tually to will the gesture. Inevitably she fails; she comes to
recognize that the "night was not impartial. No, the night
loved some more than others, served some more than others"
(p. 124).

Earlier in the story, Nina attempts to partake of myth
by following Easter into a swamp on the other side of the
lake. Upon entering the swamp, which is "all enveloping,
dark and at the same time vivid, alarming," she comes to
see Moon Lake from "a different aspect altogether" (p. 113).
But even in this primordial world, in this return to the beginning of time, Nina is unable to share in myth. She and
Easter find a boat which Nina is determined to free, but
upon pulling it out of the "sucking, minnowy mud," she finds

that the boat is chained to the shore. For Nina, unlike Mattie Will of "Sir Rabbit," there is no journey in store. As much as she desires, she cannot become a wanderer.

Only Easter and, once again, Loch are destined to take part in that special experience. Every morning all the girls are herded together to take their morning dip in the lake. Mrs. Gruenwald hoarsely sings, "Good morning, Mr. Dip, Dip, Dip, with your water just as cold as ice!" (p. 100) and, walking into the lake, she swims away. The girls feebly follow suit, but only the Morgana girls can swim, and even they do little more than stand around in the water holding onto the life rope, "hungry and waiting" until the time when Loch blows his bugle and they can all get out. Nina's sentiments express the girls' detestation of this daily ritual most clearly: "There is nobody and nothing named Mr. Dip; it is not a good morning until you have had coffee, and the water is the temperature of a just-cooling biscuit, thank Goodness" (p. 101). One morning, however, something exceptional happens. Easter climbs onto the high diving board and, waiting there, suddenly falls into the lake as Exum, a black child, gives her heel the "tenderest, obscurest little brush" (p. 125). Loch swims to the rescue, but Easter is nearly drowned by the time he reaches her, and it takes some time before he successfully resuscitates her. Meanwhile, Miss Lizzie Stark, Jinny's mother, who visits the camp daily, arrives and ineffectively orders that Loch remove himself from the drowned girl sprawled atop the picnic table, while the girls look on, aghast that life-saving is so brutal, so "much worse than they had dreamed" (p. 129).

What they are witnessing is the fulfillment of the ritual in which they have daily failed to participate. Easter has truly gone for a "dip," which archaically means "to baptize by immersion." Easter undergoes a baptism which mythologically permits the self-renewal which the name she has given herself signifies (her name is spelled Esther), and, through the girls' participation in the experience (they have no choice but to look on, and Jinny Love even participates by fanning Easter with "a persistence they had not dreamed of" [p. 131]),[16] permits their renewal as well. It allows for a new beginning, for an opening up of the minds of the girls at Moon Lake Camp to a greater awareness of life and death. What Miss Lizzie, the social leader of the community, cannot tolerate, understandably, is Loch's life-saving--which is a metaphorical acting out of a confrontation with the world outside of the community, with chaos, with death. Moreover,

symbolically the life-saving represents the sex act, the im-
plantation in Easter of a new seed of life. Now, as Nina
observes, all present partake of the time of myth: this is
a time "far, far ahead of her-- ... without time moving
any more" (p. 134). Miss Lizzie Stark's historicism has
no power here. As Parnell Moody tells her: "Can't any
of us help it, Miss Lizzie. Can't any of us. It's what he
[Loch] came for" (p. 130). Again, Nina sees things momentarily from an entirely different aspect. She faints, loses
the consciousness which has prevented her previously from
partaking of myth. By the end of the story even Jinny
thinks in terms of the future. But her prediction that Nina
and she will always be old maids is wrong. She is too much
of historical time to have vision. Nina and she turn back
from their walk to join "the singing" (p. 138), but it is clear
that their song will be dictated by the metronome.

While the girls' summer camp still contains some
possibility for myth, Morgana,. several years later, does
not. Ran MacLain, one of the twins, is now married to
Jinny Love Stark, and he has left her because she has had
an affair with Woody Spights, the story of which, as the title
of Ran's impassioned plea to his still-missing father suggests,
"the whole world knows," at least his world, the world of
Morgana. And, since the events have already been subsumed
into community history, Ran's life is taken over by the community as well. As Miss Perdita Mayo, who daily visits Ran
at work in the bank, reports:

> My Circle declares Jinny's going to divorce you,
> marry Woodrow. I said, Why? Thing of the flesh,
> I told my Circle, won't last. Sister said you'd kill
> him, and I said Sister, who are you talking about?
> If it's Ran MacLain that I knew in his buggy, I
> said, he's not at all likely to take on to that extent
> (p. 146).

But Ran is ready to kill. Trapped in space, just as Miss
Eckhart was, working in a bank cage behind bars, living in
a hot rented room in the same house where Miss Eckhart
gave piano lessons--perhaps the same room--the same house
where he grew up, and having no place to go but to drive up
and down the main street, Ran, at least imaginatively, plots
Woody's murder. His mother, Snowdie, · exhorts him to move
to MacLain, the neighboring town where she now lives, the
town where, as its name suggests, myth is still possible, but
Ran is too much in love with Jinny and all that she represents

to leave. Snowdie warns him, "Son, you're walking around in a dream" (p. 145), but Ran no longer recognizes the significance of that statement, and like Katie and Cassie before him, despairs that the world is made no clearer. He focuses all of his awareness on one event in the past: his wife's infidelity. Ran has no Virgie to help free him from his historical perspective, but he does have Maideen Sumrall, an unimaginative farm girl who has come to town to work in the Seed and Feed store. It is on her that Ran takes out his vengeance. They drive to Vicksburg, and eventually end up in a motel where Ran takes out his father's pistol and, putting the gun to his head, pulls the trigger. The gun is empty. But Maideen is not so fortunate; after the sexual encounter that follows Ran's attempted suicide, she kills herself in the store where she works. Unlike Ran, Maideen acts, and her act has significance. Her mother's maiden name is the same as Mattie Will's, Sojourner. Thus, in a small way she too is connected with myth. Her death is a sacrificial death which again permits a renewal. One discovers later that Ran, after Maideen's death, is reunited with Jinny. The farm girl's suicide even gets him elected as mayor years later. But Ran himself is lost forever to historicism. His existence, like the tale which he tells, lies already in past despair. And, as Welty implies, it is a despair which now "the whole world knows."

Certainly, Eugene, Ran's twin brother living in San Francisco, knows that despair. In "Music from Spain" Welty describes the conditions which lead him one morning to slap his wife across the face and leave the house, unconsciously seeking and finding an experience which will permit him again to share in myth. Emma, his wife, is described as a woman with a historical sensibility. She is obsessed by the death of her only child, Fan, and therefore is able to do very little in the present except sit and talk with a neighbor. Eugene himself works at the job of putting together clocks, at a job defined by clock time; waiting at the door is the jeweler's son, watching to see that no one arrives to work late. But on this special morning, Eugene slips past him and comes across the Spanish guitarist whom he and Emma had seen in concert the night before (in one of their only nights out since Fan's death). Eugene saves the guitarist from being hit by an automobile. Through that act a special kinship arises between the two of them, and Eugene and the Spaniard wander together throughout the city all day without being able to speak a word of each other's language.

If the incidents in this story seem unbelievable, it is perhaps because on this special day the events which occur to Eugene are not of that literal and historical world. To the non-visionary they appear as in a dream, but to one who partakes of myth they, like all of the events which occur in the time of myth in The Golden Apples, have great significance. For the Spaniard to whom Eugene attaches himself is another wanderer. As McHaney points out, the Spaniard's face, having "the enchanted presence of a smile on the face of a beast" (p. 173), seems to be the face which looked in at Cassie in her dreams. And, like Miss Eckhart, the guitarist plays a music from far off, some "unbearably rapid or subtle songs of this own country" (p. 183), a music "most unexpected" (p. 173) which makes Eugene feel as if on a "visit to a vast present-time" (p. 174). So it is to be expected that Eugene's journey with the guitarist to the top of a hill overlooking the ocean--where the two men battle, clinging to each other as if they were in love, and where the Spaniard lifts Eugene out over the edge of the cliff, wheeling him in air as if to throw him over before setting him down again--should end in renewal, in a "vision--some niche of clarity, some future" (pp. 197-98), some hope for him and Emma. But as with Ran, the renewal is only temporary. Returning home, Eugene is not met by Emma running to him as he has imagined she might; rather, she sits in her kitchen "talking-away" to her "great friend, Mrs. Herring from next door ..." (p. 201), and together they condemn the Spaniard for not fitting their societal requirements: for his long hair, for his laughing out loud at church where he was supposedly seen that morning with a woman by Mrs. Herring, for his "bad taste" (p. 202).

"The Wanderers" takes the reader back to Morgana where Katie Rainey, she who began the book, has just died. But Katie is not the only one to die or about to die in this story of the dead. Eugene's body has been sent back to Morgana for burial; Cassie's mother has died, committed suicide some years after her husband's death (Cassie, true to her ability only to remember, memorializes the death by spelling her mother's name in hyacinths); Miss Lizzie Stark is now an old woman, too old even to lay out Katie's body; Snowdie, who lays out the body in Lizzie's stead, is nearly seventy; and King, Zeus himself, who has come back home, is terrifying now because he is "too old" (p. 246). The whole town has radically aged. The road by which Katie waited--where she waited like all the town's old people," ... watching and waiting for something they didn't really know

any longer, wouldn't recognize to see it coming in the road"
(p. 205), where she waited out her "remaining space of time"
(a metaphor which clearly defines time as linear) (p. 206)--
that road, everyone says, now "goes the wrong way," which
means only that the "wrong people" go by on it, those "riding
trucks, very fast or heavily loaded, and carrying blades and
chains, to chop and haul trees" (p. 213) as they deplete Morgan's Woods. In other words, the old myths and their incar-
nations and even their sacred places [17] have fallen, and those
who perceived only in terms of history have become history
themselves, are replaced by a people who move faster, who
are more able to try to outrun time than Katie, who tries
once more, however, just before her death by listing "faster
and faster" all the flowers she can think of (pp. 207-08).

Thus Virgie is alone in a house of dead people, alone
in the midst of almost all of those who come to the wake
and funeral, and who keep her from partaking even of that
last ritual left her, death itself. They fondle her, reassure
her, protect her as they have always, but for Virgie as well
as the reader they are now only ghosts. As Juba, Miss
Lizzie's black servant, sent to help Virgie, says: "I seen
more ghosts than live peoples, round here. Black and white.
I seen plenty both. Miss Virgie, some is given to see, some
try but is not given" (p. 237). Only King shows vestiges of
life. While all listen to the funeral music, he pushes out
his "stained lip" and makes a "hideous face at Virgie, like
a silent yell. It was a yell at everything--including death,
not leaving it out--and he did not mind taking his present
animosity out on Virgie Rainey; indeed, he chose her" (p. 227).

King chooses Virgie because he knows that she is
one "given to see," that only she can understand that his
hideous face is made from the horror and anger that he
knows since he can no longer partake of myth. It is a face
that Virgie sees and carries with her, not in her dreams,
but in her awakened and active mind. After the wake, Virgie
crosses the road to the old MacLain place and walks back
into the pasture down to the river. She undresses and lets
herself into the water, where after a few moments she hangs
"suspended in felicity" (p. 219). Thus she purifies herself;
she is reborn, which in this book of myths one has seen
occur time and again. She is now free to lead the life of
a wanderer. After the funeral, she packs, gets into her
car and drives to MacLain (still the town connected with
myth) and, as it begins to rain, stands under a tree where
she suddenly remembers Miss Eckhart and her lessons. But

what Virgie most remembers is a picture which hung in the studio, Perseus with the head of Medusa. What Virgie perceives about the picture is not merely the heroic act, the act of order which makes visible "a horror in life ... a horror in love ... the separateness," but, because Virgie "sees things in their time," because, the reader is told, "she must believe in the Medusa equally with Perseus," Virgie sees the "stroke of the sword in three moments," which occur over and over again in time like music: "Every time Perseus struck off the Medusa's head, there was the beat of time, and the melody. Endless the Medusa, and Perseus endless" (p. 243). In other words, because she sees things not as in a dream, but recognizes and accepts things in their multitudinousness, she sees life in all of its fullness: in the past, present and the future simultaneously. And, seeing that, the very structure of time is revealed to her; it is revealed that time is cyclical; as Welty says (not of life, however, but of Intruder in the Dust), life is "full of riddles and always starting over."[18] As Virgie waits under that tree with an old black beggar woman, it is no longer certain whether she will leave or stay. It does not matter. For Virgie, unlike anyone else in the book--except perhaps for Loch on that one summer afternoon--has in that revelation learned how to wander without moving. Remaining where she stands, Virgie listens to the "magical percussion":

> ... the running of the horse and the bear, the stroke of the leopard, the dragon's crusty slither, and the glimmer and the trumpet of the swan (p. 244),

a world where history is embraced by myth.

Notes

[1] Thomas L. McHaney, "Eudora Welty and the Multitudinous Golden Apples," Mississippi Quarterly, XXVI (Fall 1973), 589.

[2] Most notably, Harry C. Morris, "Eudora Welty's Use of Mythology," Shenandoah, VI (Spring 1955), 34-40; Ruth M. Vande Kieft, Eudora Welty (New York: Twayne, 1962); and, F. D. Carson, "'The Song of the Wandering Aengus': Allusion in The Golden Apples," Notes on Mississippi Writers, VI (Spring 1973), 14-17.

[3]I must emphasize that I am using the word "history" here in its most limited meaning. History, understood properly, is also a thing of flux; the historian is as much a creator as the artist. But here I am using the word "history" to suggest a sensibility which, looking to the past, sees time as progression, as spatialized.

[4]Actually, the events narrated by Katie Rainey in "Shower of Gold" begin much earlier than this time-span. She reports that her husband Fate claims he saw King MacLain riding in the inauguration parade with Governor Vardaman to the new capitol building. The new capitol was dedicated on June 4, 1903, and Vardaman was elected governor in September of the same year. However, the work actually "begins" a few days after the Halloween day when the MacLain twins frighten away their father and Katie's daughter, Virgie, swallows a button. By the end of the book, Virgie is in her forties.

[5]There is also a desire to share in King's "History," however. Later in the book the reader is told that King has given Katie the chair on which she sits; thus, he made her a queen on a throne.

[6]Welty, The Golden Apples (New York: Harcourt, Brace, 1949), p. 3. All further references are to this edition.

[7]Vande Kieft, p. 113. Harry C. Morris was, to my knowledge, the first critic to note that the Zeus-Danaë myth is at work in The Golden Apples.

[8]Zelma Turner Howard, The Rhetoric of Eudora Welty's Short Stories (Jackson: University and College Press of Mississippi, 1973), pp. 102-120.

[9]This idea is emphasized by the fact that, when Miss Eckhart is raped by a black, the community cannot fathom why she does not move away. Again, by staying, Miss Eckhart reminds them of another reality, of a danger outside the community order.

[10]Mircea Eliade describes just such a ritual in his Myth and Reality (New York: Harper, 1963), pp. 50-53. He calls it the "perfection of the beginnings," for in the myth the "flux of Time implies an ever greater distance from the 'beginnings.' and hence loss of the original perfection." This

implies a complementary idea, he suggests, "That, for something genuinely new to begin, the vestiges and the ruins of the old cycle must be completely destroyed."

[11] McHaney, p. 597.

[12] The reader is later told that Loch has moved to New York.

[13] This accords with Eliade's comments, Myth and Reality, pp. 85-91.

[14] Vande Kieft, p. 115.

[15] Jinny was much younger than both Virgie and Cassie on that rainy day when Miss Eckhart played a sonata.

[16] It should be remembered that, on that day when Miss Eckhart played a sonata, Jinny came forward and turned the pages as her teacher played.

[17] Morgan's Woods was the location of "Sir Rabbit," and functions throughout The Golden Apples as a sacred place.

[18] Welty, "In Yoknapatawpha," Hudson Review, I (Winter 1949), 596.

LOOKING DOWN FROM A HIGH PLACE:
The Serenity of Miss Welty's Losing Battles*

by M. E. Bradford

The gifted company of artists who in the past four
decades overcame the logic of their times and gave a serious,
indigenous literature to the American South is now, for the
most part, dispersed. And the few of their number who remain alive write, Robert Penn Warren excepted, less and
less. Even the so-called "second-generation" grows old,
less numerous, and silent. [1] Therefore a new novel by one
of the progenitors--a major effort after fifteen years--is by
definition an event: a changing and completion for the total
shape, the proportions, of this unusual phase in the history
of modern letters. [2] A respectful awareness of what Eudora
Welty has accomplished and of her place as a central figure
in the Southern Renaissance inevitably conditions our recep-
tion of her new opus. And it should. For Losing Battles
draws upon the resources of its kindred predecessors among
Southern books and is on its face an allusion to the corpus
of Renaissance fiction: both to earlier creations by Miss
Welty and to the work of her peers, both in theme and in
form. Indeed, as does any artifact produced within the con-
fines of an established literary tradition, this novel insists
that it be read with its given milieu in mind.

The rich texture of Losing Battles presents special
problems to the critic. Probably its overall effect is to
divert the careful reader's attention away from the fable by
which its steady and vital flow is sustained, a tactic often
used by Miss Welty in her short stories. Yet there is an
action in this novel, an action familiar to those who have

*Reprinted by permission of the author and publisher from
RANAM (Recherches Anglaises et Américaines), Vol. IV
(1971), 92-97.

read William Faulkner, Caroline Gordon, Katherine Anne
Porter, Andrew Lytle, and Allen Tate. With a description
of that "movement of the spirit" and of its causes, formal
critical consideration must begin.

The issue in Losing Battles is, in a word, cultural
survival: whether or not a yeoman, hill country version of
the familiar order that was the South (despite some confusion
over Negroes) can absorb and adjust to an alien pressure;
whether, and, if so, how?[3] The governing presences here
are all women: Mrs. Beulah Renfro (the matriarchal extension of her Grandmother Vaughn, whose ninetieth birthday
is the book's time and whose old, plain, and rambling home
is its setting); Miss Julia Mortimer, the village schoolmarm
and the antagonist of all that is meant by Vaughn, Renfro,
and Beecham (the divisions of the family); and, finally, young
Gloria Short Renfro, Beulah's daughter-in-law, wife to Jack
(the "hope" of the Renfro clan), and Miss Mortimer's chosen
successor as bringer of light into Banner's complacent darkness (p. 244). As had old Granny Vaughn in her time and
Beulah (or Miss Mortimer) in the present, Gloria must de-
cide "how it will be."[4] And, even before the narrative begins, even before her Jack returns from the penitentiary
year he spent for her and family's sake, Gloria has in her
own way chosen. In loving Jack, she disappoints Miss Mortimer; yet, as she informs the Renfros on every opportunity,
she will not be another Beulah, will not "disappear" in a
role (pp. 171, 268, 315). While she awaits her husband's
coming from Parchman, Mississippi's great outdoor farm
prison, we are belabored with the fact of her identity and
with its importance to what that recovery will mean. But
if Miss Mortimer (qua "uplift" as principle) and the forces
personified in Beulah (will-to-be-family or prescription) will
not have the victory, neither will Gloria's desire for a private existence with Jack and their children (pp. 320, 435).
Jack makes that much unmistakable. The injustice of his
year in prison, his bad taste of the great world, has somewhat circumscribed his boyhood innocence. More "education"
follows hard after his arrival in Banner. Yet he is now the
Renfro, the centerpiece and lifegiver for all who share his
blood. And he accepts that place as an a priori fact, accepts it despite disappointment at the loss of his horse, his
truck, or his simple notion of physical pride: even if he
cannot have his planned revenge on Curly, his local Nemesis,
or upon the Miss Mortimer-trained county judge who first
sentenced him for assault upon said Curly (pp. 362, 434).
For he now has an identity in both love and duty--is yet

affirming it as they make love for the first time since their separation (pp. 361-62) and later as they head home together (at the book's end), she riding the horse he leads and Jack singing the old Southern folk hymn, "Bringing in the Sheaves." This harvest will be partial, unequal to the long planting (or to the great tree, major symbol of the novel, which presides over their reunion). For Miss Julia, incarnation of modernity on the march, has had some effect. And there will never be, therefore, another day like this one for "the family." Everyone loses a little. Yet there will come a "harvest" and a season for rejoicing (p. 436).

As we might expect, much of the early comment on Losing Battles shows a misconception of the pattern I have just described. The trouble was, of course, Miss Julia. [5] Being children of our times, the reviewers could find no other character in the novel with whom they might comfortably identify, no one operating within the book by whom they could measure the action there unfolded--that is, without surrendering part of their identity as heirs of the Enlightenment. In the 1930s the Julia Mortimers of the South were coming into their own. By 1941 the presiding figures of the region were less and less certainly the heads of landed families, political spokesmen, lawyers, and clergy. Teachers-- with the support of business and professional men whom they had helped to train, plus a new breed of journalist, and the ubiquitous helpful "outside" visitors--rose to be figures of reference and instruments of alteration. Everyone cried out for the public school, even though the South had always been slow to kindle with this New England enthusiasm for the Faustian; and no one cried out more vocally than the prototypes of Miss Welty's confused reviewers, be they home grown, like Judge Moody, or "imported," like the founders of the Normals (colleges of education) where schoolmarms were manufactured out of ex-Presbyterian girls with a secularized eschatology. But Eudora Welty is old enough and perceptive enough to know her world both ways: wise enough to know that most monomaniacal efforts to "make the world better" (p. 250) do not secure the results intended.

Julia Mortimer's role in Miss Welty's new work is, therefore, clearly hedged by and enmeshed in comedy. Furthermore, despite hieratic or honorific touches underlining her portrait, that astonishing lady is made to complete the gentle and affectionate satire of her career by adding a self-judgment. Hers is one comedy among many, though sharper than the rest. The evidence of the text is plain. The mood, here as elsewhere, is elegiac. I shall explain.

First of all, a number of Miss Julia's former students speak of her as an "inspiration" (p. 244). Her impact, on girls especially, was to encourage them to play St. George to the dragon Ignorance, to live up to their private intellectual and moral potential, and then (alone) escape the smothering matrix of family and the dead hand of the past: escape in order to impose themselves upon a piece of creation with the shining vesture of learning and words for their own sake as an excuse. That is, she directed them to emulate her own triumph in that paradigmatic moment when a pupil of her school (Gloria) "spells down" the members of the lower house of the Mississippi state legislature (p. 242). Miss Julia's ultimate vision is of a world of individuals who are uninhibited in their self-perfecting and good works: uninhibited because they are unrestricted by entangling alliances which might obscure their vision of perfection to come. All of this impersonal will-to-progress is specified in the references to Miss Mortimer's missionary heritage, to her sale of the family home "behind her," to her desire to be buried under the very threshold of Banner School, to the wooden admonition of her letters, her ungracious social habits, and her other crotchets Such a teacher is certainly the harbinger of death for the communal place-rooted and time-ignoring life of Banner, an augury of the bourgeois and idealist-rationalist atomization of modern commercial and industrial civilization. She is a splendid woman--a marvel to all who know her (and a great waste as spinster in the eyes of the ladies of her county). And, as her burial on the day following the reunion indicates, she did leave a substantial intellectual progeny. But these are not in or of Banner. For the time, her people (and we can call them this, despite their differences) resist and absorb her. She will rest in their midst, pitied, in the Banner graveyard with the elders and founders of the local "tribes." Moreover, Miss Julia halfway understands why. Her last words are in a deathbed letter to Judge Moody. There she admits that, in order to be themselves, in order to survive as they understand their identity (and they can conceive of no other), her pupils were obliged to resist her (p. 298). Therefore she calls her "failure" good, for pupil and teacher. For she has herself lived only by inspiration (p. 298)--a courageous will to survive in her function or without it: "... the side that gets licked gets to the truth first. When the battle is over, something may down those with no help from the teacher, no help from the pupil, and no help from the book" (p. 298). In this, her wisdom is one with that of Beulah Renfro: the chief business of life is "standing it" (p. 360).

The title for this essay should by now be intelligible.
Losing Battles is indeed an elegiac novel. And the elegiac
as a mode of aesthetic perception invariably rests upon an
affirmation of good losing: Upon defeats like Jack's, in going
to prison to pay for--as he understands after the fact--his
Uncle Mason's murder of one Dearman (the enterprising, and
ultra-modern despoiler of the county, both land and people;
and the probable father of Gloria); defeats like Judge Moody's
when he realizes that he needs the Beecham-Renfro connection (to recover his car and to "forgive" him by not forgiving
him for Jack's incarceration) as much as they need him; defeats like weather and soil and poverty and stubborn ignorance,
as they encroach upon Banner. In the elegiac, wisdom is
spawned out of hard truth. Then it is quietly and yet affec-
tionately affirmed. The human lot, beneath the noise of pol-
itics or intellectual, religious, and economic change, remains
constant. And the instruments we can find for dealing with
it, in joy and resignation, are the old ones: honor, courage,
charity, honesty, loyalty, and memory. Love likewise keeps
a place here, and also family, which is its natural issue.
(It is significant that the author dedicates this book to the
memory of her brothers.) In this connection, work and a
little hope make sense--as do even education and the multi-
plication of words. But to remember Captain Billy Bangs,
the eldest of the Banner elders, if the world be "round and
spinning," it is possible to be overimpressed by those facts
(p. 24). His words are heavy when he mocks Miss Julia for
schooling him in such undeniable fact. Yet he calls her
"daughter."

What the texture of Losing Battles adds in support of
the pattern I have here been describing is authority· purchase
by way of a masterful employment of the serio-comic tone.
Comic, I say, but not ironic as with cosmic or philosophic
irony. The initial lushness of early pages is consciously
overdone. [6] Miss Welty's manner, in confronting the Creation, says "yes" to the "given." Her imagination is the sub-
missive, observing faculty which, years ago, Donald Davidson
identified as the informing characteristic of the new Southern
literature. To use Allen Tate's term, it is not of the "an-
gelic" order, not bent upon remaking. Miss Welty offers
no cures. Before her memories she submits in order to
recover the meaningful shape of a history she has experienced.
She does not tell us "how" about anything. From her high
perspective, it is clear that such lofty enterprises are to no
purpose. The "what" of things is of more importance. These
she does not mistake.

Notes

[1] I speak of such authors as Peter Taylor, Walter
Sullivan, William Humphrey, Ovid Williams Pierce, Madison
Jones, Walker Percy, Jesse Stuart, and Reynolds Price.
Flannery O'Connor, James Agee, and Randall Jarrell are,
of course, prematurely silent by reason of their death. Guy
Owens, George Garrett, and William Styron do not quite be-
long inside the tradition, though they may, for particular
works, be included. Likewise the poet James Dickey and
the poet-novelist John Corrington. (Some of these people,
it may be argued, are "third generation".)

[2] Losing Battles (New York: Random House, 1970).

[3] In a fundamental sense, the entire South was a family
rather than a regime or state (as the political philosophers
speak of these things). Seen in terms of one or another of
its characteristic gestures, it could be called either patriar-
chal or matriarchal. Moreover, as Andrew Lytle has insisted, particular families were "the institution of Southern
life" (The Hero with the Private Parts [Baton Rouge: The
Louisiana State University Press, 1966], p. 76). The Beecham-
Renfro clan, in the framework of Banner, is therefore a
suitable illustration of the regional macrocosm. The members have no full identity outside of the connection (p. 346).
They live by memory and periodically celebrate their oneness
in such sacramental ceremonies as reunion, marriage, and
burial. They keep no law above the prescription of group
memory (p. 325). The recitation of that memory is, as we
would expect, part of each of their gatherings (p. 180 et seq.).
And, of course, the events of this birthday-homecoming-reunion
become part of the story, and as Uncle Noah Webster observes,
are "... never to be forgotten" (p. 354). The point of all
this use of family as paradigm would be lost if Blacks had
a part in this book because their presence would have di-
verted critic and reader from its meaning. For the South
had a familial character from its founding, and before Blacks
were introduced there (cf. Richard Weaver's many studies of
the regional mind for documentation).

[4] Women are the particular repositories of the Southern
pieties. Along with place (see Miss Welty's maps), they an-
chor a society. (Eudora Welty's famous disquisition, "Place
in Fiction," appeared in South Atlantic Quarterly, LV [Jan-
uary, 1956], 57-72). Beulah Renfro cannot imagine why
Judge Moody knows so much of Miss Mortimer unless he

"aspired" to her or was her kin. As for men, Beulah adds, they "... don't realize anything" (p. 199). In this she resembles the oracular ladies of Delta Wedding (New York: Harcourt Brace, 1946). Assuredly, this new novel is, like the tale of "Shellmound," a "woman's book. "

[5]As representative of these reviews, I cite Louis D. Rubin's "Everything Brought Out in the Open: Eudora Welty's Losing Battles," Hollins Critic, VIII (June, 1970), 1-12. Rubin insists that Miss Julia teaches Banner folk "the ultimate consequences of their humanity. " Infinitely superior to this reflexive modernism is Lewis Simpson's "The Chosen People," in Southern Review, VI (Summer, 1970), xvii, xix, xxi-xxiii.

[6]A thorough reading of Losing Battles would concentrate on the novel's slow unfolding and upon the role of conversation--tale telling--as a vehicle for rendering action within that unfolding.

CIRCLING-IN:
The Concept of the Home in Eudora Welty's
Losing Battles and The Optimist's Daughter

by William McMillen

      Eudora Welty believes that the concept of place is of
primary concern--as primary as plot or character--in the
art of her fiction. "The truth is," she has written, "fiction
depends for its life on place. Location is the cross roads
of circumstance, the proving ground of 'What happened?
Who's here? Who's coming?'--and that is the heart's field."[1]
Most of her "heart's field" is firmly set in the hills and trace
and delta of Mississippi. Her dependence on, and use of,
place is often cited as one of the most noticeable Southern
characteristics of her work. Elmo Howell in a recent article links Welty's concern for place with a host of other Southern writers, all of whom have learned to depend on the history and characteristics embedded in the soil of the South.[2]
Welty, herself, emphasizes the concrete importance of place.
Her essay "Some Notes on Time in Fiction" first establishes
time and place as "the two bases of reference upon which the
novel, in seeking to come to grips with human experience,
must depend for its validity...."[3] While time, for her, is
abstract and fluid, place provides the balance by being concrete:

> ... place has surface, which will take the imprint
> of man--his hand, his foot, his mind; it can be
> tamed, domesticized. It has shape, size, bound-
> aries; man can measure himself against them.[4]

This concept of place becomes almost a romanticized pioneer
ideal--man against the great but yielding earth. Yet Welty's
fiction is about discovering new selves, not new lands. Her
characters, not place, propel her fiction. It is necessary
then to look at what, or more properly where, her characters envision place to be and what they envision place to represent.

In much of Welty's fiction, place has come to mean the concept of home. Home is the man-made extension of the land. Like the land itself, it is shaped by man's hand and is used to establish certain boundaries. Most importantly, however, it retains natural physical attributes. The homes in both Losing Battles and The Optimist's Daughter are described over and over again with imagery which draws nature and the home together. The focus of the first paragraph of Losing Battles is to establish the natural harmony of the Renfro-Vaughn homestead: "Then as if something came sliding out of the sky, the whole tin roof of the house ran with the new blue. "[5] Welty takes us from the moon through the ridges and hills of Banner to the small house. We go right down to the smallest detail of how the "Cannas came around the house on either side in a double row, like the Wall of Jericho, with their blooms unfurled ... " (5).

Similarly, the McKelva home in The Optimist's Daughter, although in a much less rural setting than Losing Battles, is consistently associated with the nature that immediately surrounds it. As we first approach the house, nature even seems to acknowledge our presence and Laurel's return: "Laurel saw that the daffodils were in bloom, long streamers of them reaching down the yard, hundreds of small white trumpets. "[6] The daffodils, like the cannas above, present an almost formal welcome to the novel's characters. Later, Laurel tends to the flowers that surround her home, working "among the iris that still held a ragged line along the back of the house up to the kitchen door" (105). And, near the end of the novel: "From the stair window she could see that the crabapple tree had rushed into green, all but one sleeve that was still flowery" (170).

What is initially, and throughout the novels firmly, established is that the homes are natural places built by men and women who strove to be in harmony with nature. Homes become the natural symbol of the taming and domestication of the land. They are the sturdy products of such strong-willed characters as Granny Vaughn and Judge McKelva. Yet Granny and the Judge are not the central characters of their respective novels. Those roles are reserved for their children and grandchildren. Might the concept of home change in the succeeding generations? Could the sons and daughters not only be out of touch with the natural harmony of home but even at odds with its demands? I believe the home becomes the symbol and focus of the younger generation's rebellion from the family influence and also from the influence of the past.

Welty's rebellious younger generations are most commonly identified by the Ruth Vande Kieft term "Wanderers" (from the Welty story "The Wanderers" in The Golden Apples). These characters are forced by circumstances to come to the realization that in order to be free they must strike-out on their own, breaking all relationship with the home, their family and their past. It doesn't matter where these characters go (or even if they physically leave by the end of their stories) as long as they recognize the need to go. It is significant that the wanderers often come to their awarenesses during ritualistic, family home celebrations. Virgie Rainey's sudden understanding during her mother's funeral in The Golden Apples is perhaps the prime example of a wanderer's sudden awareness. Yet both Losing Battles and The Optimist's Daughter also have family celebrations which result in the creation of wanderers.

Symbolically, these celebrations, whether they are the happy reunion or the unhappy funeral, are the last grasp of the past over the lives of the younger generations. Losing Battles and The Optimist's Daughter both have dead or dying characters like Julia Mortimer and the half-senile Granny Vaughn who, along with hazy characters like the war victim Sam Dale Beecham, attempt to wield power over the young vibrant lives of Gloria and Jack Renfro. Likewise, the strong Judge McKelva and the ghostly figures of his dead wife and Laurel's dead husband control the life of Laurel.

Both novels have the strength of the dead's power coming from their hold on the home and the place. Granny's birthday is the reunion when all the family gathers at her homestead. Julia Mortimer for years had a map in her schoolroom defining the boundaries she wanted her students to conquer. Judge McKelva maintains his control even after death by being displayed not in a funeral home but in the old-fashion Presbyterian tradition of his own front parlor. Even in burial he takes a commanding position over the land with others of his generation:

> The top of the hill ahead was crowded with winged angels and life-sized effigies of bygone citizens in old-fashioned dress, standing as if by count among the columns and shafts and conifers ... embarked on a voyage that is always returning in dreams (89).

And, finally, it is Julia Mortimer's last and unfulfilled wish

that she be buried under the schoolhouse stoop so that each
succeeding generation will have to literally pass over her
memory.

But our concern in these two novels is ultimately not
with the dead but, as Gloria reminds us halfway through
Losing Battles, with the living (162). We must recognize
the struggles of the living to come to grips with not only
the human past but also the home as an on-going physical
symbol of the past. Homes become the holders of memories,
storehouses which have an almost magical power to attract
the families. The faithful return of the Renfro-Vaughn Beecham clan is a prime example. The real proof of the holding power of the clan, however, is the members' unfaltering
faith in Jack's return from the prison farm. Although they
know he is not scheduled for release, they also believe that
nothing can keep him from Granny's birthday and reunion.
The very pull of the house will bring him home. Therefore,
when he appears, the house itself rumbles in anticipation:

> ... the floor drummed and swayed, a pan dropped
> from its nail in the kitchen wall, and overhead even
> the tin roof seemed to quiver with a sound like all
> the family spoons set to jingling in their glass (71).

Significantly, Jack's first words are not about or to his wife,
or even his family. Instead, he cries, "'A new roof! I
could see it a mile coming!'" (73). The old homestead has
acted as a beacon to guide Jack home.

Gloria's struggle in Losing Battles, then, is to capture her young husband from the grips of not only his family
but also his physical home. Gloria is an orphan, a person
without family or home. She has been given shelter by each
of the antagonistic sides in the novel in turn. First Julia
Mortimer attempted to make her into the schoolteacher who
would take over the Banner school from Julia. But Gloria
rejected Julia to marry Jack. However, since Jack almost
immediately went to the prison farm after their marriage,
she found herself in the center of a second family situation.
Her stay in the Renfro home was a constant struggle to maintain her independence despite the family's effort to integrate
her into their structure and ways. But she resists, often
going to the edge of the property to sit by the Chinaberry
trees looking away from the home.

The family, however, buoyed by Jack's predicted

return, goes all out to claim Gloria as one of their own. They try to make her a blood-member "cousin" despite evidence that her supposed father (Sam Dale Beecham) was sterile from a childhood accident with fire. Besides raising this mental doubt, the family physically attempts to make Gloria say "Beecham" (instead of Uncle) in a vicious watermelon fight. Significantly, her tormentors are led by Aunts who have all married into the family and have given up their own identities and freedom. When they finally challenge Gloria about the future, she can only say that she and Jack and their baby will face the unknown, "And she looked out to see the distance, but beyond the bright porch she couldn't see anything at all" (320).

Laurel McKelva is also facing an unknown which is tempered by the home that she must look through and beyond. She knows that the future will be changed by her father's death and this final dissolution of her small family. Cleanth Brooks points out in his essay on The Optimist's Daughter how the family home, the physical symbol of Laurel's past, has already undergone changes wrought by Judge McKelva's shrewish second wife, Fay: "As she [Laurel] wanders through it [the home], she cannot help noticing the little changes in decoration, the tell-tale rearrangements of furniture and objects, that speak of the new wife and of the Judge's closing years."[7] Fay has lived in the Judge's house but is insensitive to any value other than its monetary worth. She is unaffected and unsympathetic to the home's drawing and holding power. Likewise, Fay's family, the Chisoms, away from their own Texas home, view the Judge's house as a monstrosity ("'It'd make a good boardinghouse ...'"). Yet Fay herself is mindlessly drawn to her home and impulsively leaves for Texas as soon as the Judge is buried.

Laurel thus is left alone for one final stay in her family home. Her desire to find the past, to escape Fay's superficial changes, leads her upstairs as if she is circling-in on the very heart of her home, her family and her past. This climactic crisis chapter of the novel begins with an invocation by the house itself, "Windows and door alike were singing, buffeted by the storm" (130). The storm continues throughout the entire chapter and night as Laurel's turmoil builds up against her house of memories. She first goes into her parent's bedroom and then into the small sewing room off the bedroom, the room that had originally been her nursery.

> ... she had to feel about for a lamp. She turned
> it on: her old student gooseneck lamp on a low
> table. By its light she saw that here was where
> her mother's secretary had been exiled, and her
> own study table, the old slipper chair; there was
> the brassbound three-layer trunk; there was the
> sewing machine (132).

All these physical objects of the home itself together in this
small warm interior room bring the past flooding over Laurel.

The secretary is pigeonholed with letters from Laurel's
father to her mother. As she reads the letters, she moves
from her parents' relationship to her own youth and her visits
with relatives. Then her mother's illness and blindness are
relived while the house and storm around her keep pace with
her thoughts: "What burdens we lay on the dying, Laurel
thought, as she listened now to the accelerated rain on the
roof ... " (146). Laurel's most painful realization is that
her own mother had gone through much the same crisis of
home and family, past and future, that Laurel now faces.
Her mother, however, died blind, ignorant of Laurel's and
the Judge's love. After a final stroke, she lay in her bed
believing that she "was neither home nor 'up home,' that she
was left among strangers ... " (151). With the final realization of all this grief of the living, Laurel has a vision of
her dead husband. The vision is of Phil demanding life.
Yet Laurel knows that his life, indeed all of her past, is
lost except to her memory. Thus, while she weeps finally
for what happened to life, her husband's cry for life echoes
around the house:

> His voice rose with the wind in the night and went
> around the house and around the house. It became
> a roar. 'I wanted it.' (155)

The result of Laurel's night of memories is that she
is freed of their hold on her life. This is not to say that
she has forgotten them but the paralysis which they have imposed on her, the fact, for example, that she has not remar-
ried, is gone. The remaining few pages of the novel are
filled with her discarding the now useless physical symbols
of her memories. The next day (a beautiful, clear day)
Laurel burns her mother's letters and her own school note-
books gathered from the sewing room. Later, she fights
momentarily for her mother's breadboard before giving it

up to Fay (who has just returned from Texas) and back to the house: "'Never mind,' said Laurel, laying the breadboard down on the table where it belonged. 'I think I can get along without that too'" (179). Laurel then leaves her home with a mad dash out the front door to a car filled with her "brides-maids" who will take her to her train. The scene is a repe-tition of her wedding day but now, unlike then, she is com-pletely free of her home and past.

The conclusion of Losing Battles has Jack and Gloria also moving away from the dead and toward a new life. They momentarily attend Julia Mortimer's funeral but are obviously out of place: "'I don't think they've got any business at a funeral,'" says one very old mourner (429). They leave and discover that they are possessionless but they are also free for the first time. The three of them, Jack, Gloria and their baby, are joined by Jack's horse, a symbol of their ability to start over, working the soil. Jack ends the novel singing a hymn of hope and plenty, "Bringing in the Sheaves."

In both Losing Battles and The Optimist's Daughter, the homes are finally abandoned to the families and the past. The idea of place has not necessarily been lost by the younger generations; but a sense of freedom has been gained. Jack and Gloria are not going to leave Banner, and Laurel will return to Mount Salus to visit friends. But the paralyzing holding power of the home has been set aside. The ideal of place, the comfort of the house and the familiarity of the house "things" have conspired with the older generation to hold the younger characters of the novels.

When Jack returns from the prison, he mentions pri-vately to Gloria how old the family now appears. Yet he is simultaneously attracted to the stability and even the newness (the tin roof) of the family home. It is the realization of Jack and Gloria and Laurel McKelva that their homes are only physical containers of the past. When they can leave home, they are free of their memories and free to face a new future.

Notes

[1] "Place in Fiction," South Atlantic Quarterly, 55 (January 1956), 59.

[2] "Eudora Welty and the Use of Place in Southern Fiction," Arizona Quarterly 28 (Autumn 1972), 248-56.

[3] The Mississippi Quarterly 4 (Autumn 1973), 483.

[4] Ibid.

[5] Losing Battles (New York: Random House, 1970), 4. Subsequent references in the text are to this edition.

[6] The Optimist's Daughter (New York: Ramdom House, 1972), 51. Subsequent references in the text are to this edition.

[7] "The Past Reexamined: The Optimist's Daughter," The Mississippi Quarterly, p. 581.

PATTERN AND VISION IN THE OPTIMIST'S DAUGHTER

by John F. Desmond

If it is possible to speak of the culminating work in a great writer's canon, then Eudora Welty's The Optimist's Daughter should hold that distinction among her many masterpieces. Of all her brilliant short stories and novels, The Optimist's Daughter best focuses the unique vision of reality she has attempted to articulate throughout her long career, and in no other single work has that vision been rendered in such consummate form. Perhaps the novel's clarity stems from the fact that Welty has chosen as her primary subject, vision itself--the whole range of perception and blindness, feeling and insensitivity we see depicted through the McKelva family, their Mt. Salus neighbors, and the Chisoms in the events precipitated by Judge McKelva's death. With vision itself as subject, working reflexively as it were, the novel becomes a brilliant kaleidoscope of all those major themes that have concerned Welty for almost forty years.

Throughout her fiction Welty has frequently presented the life struggle in terms of a dynamic, rhythmic battle between order and spontaneity, between the human need to pattern experience and the vital, erupting forces which, for better or worse, shatter the human design. In The Optimist's Daughter, Welty explores this theme by examining the mysterious relationship between memory and experience. Paradoxically, memory gives order and pattern to experience (though often an erroneous or idealized order), yet this order is constantly being disrupted by experience, a violation which in turn may nevertheless be life-giving. Memory too is life-giving insofar as it gives intelligible pattern and felt meaning to the raw shocks of experience. And the manner in which this relationship can be either static or dynamic is a crucial problem Welty explores in the novel. For the relationship between memory and experience, examined through the con-

sciousness of her protagonist Laurel McKelva Hand, is inti-
mately linked with several other familiar Welty concerns:
the mystery of the private and the public self, the theme of
the wanderers and the attachment to home, and that most
pervasive of Weltian themes, the mystery of love and separateness, sustenance and violation which she sees at the heart
of all human relationships.

What makes The Optimist's Daughter such a remark-
able achievement is that Welty's thematic concerns serve as
formal, organizing principles in the structure of the novel.
For example, the fact that Laurel's interior life is largely
kept hidden from us throughout the first two-thirds of the
novel is a direct reflection of the extreme privacy she maintains. Conversely, the gaudy public nature of Judge McKelva's funeral serves appropriately to define important aspects
of his character and reveal its weaknesses. On a broader
scale, Welty's structural technique of shifting between raw
experience and memory, past and present, corresponds perfectly to the dynamic interaction between them she wishes to
represent. In brief, as the novel progresses the formal
structure itself resolves the very issues about experience
raised by the novel--resolves them in the sense of providing
a dramatic, intelligible pattern--so that the reader experiences a kind of "double effect" which enhances the power of
the novel immeasurably.

Within these larger structural patterns Welty brilliantly
weaves a set of image patterns which I shall identify and later
attempt to show their development in the novel. The first
has to do with images of patterns themselves, images of ordering, seen for example in Laurel's career as designer of
fabrics, in her mother's love of sewing, in Phil Hand's career as designer and maker, and most importantly, in the
very acts of reflection and memory, themselves faculties for
ordering perception and experience. The reverse of this pattern is epitomized, of course, by Fay Chisom, who is "unpredictable," a blunderer who is both incapable of making
anything and of ordering experience through reflection, who
scorns memory and the past. A second pattern has to do
with images of birds, especially the key image of the two
pigeons feeding each other, and the image of birds trans-
formed and distanced in Laurel's crucial vision while passing over the Mississippi and Ohio Rivers. Also, there are
Laurel's curious but revealing nickname, "Polly," her mother's
ineffective birdfrighteners and the swooping cardinals and
mockingbirds, and finally, the "irrational" chimney swift

who drives Laurel toward her night of painful but blessed
revelation. A third pattern has to do with images of food
and feeding, evoking the sustenance/violation paradox in human relationships. In addition to the crucial scene involving
the two pigeons, there are also the elaborate social ritual
of the funeral buffet, the importance of Becky as cook and
maker of bread, the gift of pecans brought to Laurel by
Grandpa Chisom, and conversely, Fay's inability to cook,
her starved expression, the intimation that she probably was
undernourished as a child and the description of her during
the funeral as "needing a good meal."

A fourth pattern has to do with images of water, the
most important of which is Laurel's crucial "bridge" scene
above the confluence of the rivers just before her marriage.
But there are also Phil Hand's death by water and fire,
Beck's heroic river journey to Baltimore with her dying
father, Judge McKelva's flood control project, and the small
"boat" of polished river stone given by the Judge to Becky,
the one family treasure Laurel keeps at the end of the novel.
The pattern is also reflected in minor ways: Mr. Chisom
"died wanting water," and in the New Orleans hospital the
Dalzells threaten to "feed" their dying grandfather by forcibly pouring water down his throat. A fifth pattern has to
do with images of fire. Laurel associates her mother's sewing room with fire and warmth; Becky built a fire on the raft
taking her sick father to Baltimore, and later the old West
Virginia homestead burned down, through Becky risked her
life to save the Dickens collection. Throughout Judge Mc-
Kelva's funeral constant attention is given to the fire, and
before her final departure from Mt. Salus, Laurel burns her
mother's letters to her father. Finally, there is an elaborate pattern of images concerning physical touch--hands--sig-
nifying the bonds of loyalty, giving, and trust, or contrarily,
of selfish grasping, between people. Laurel's husband's sur-
name, his careful construction by hand of the breadboard for
Becky, his devoted teaching of Laurel to draw patterns, Laurel's job as designer, her desperate attempt to save her dying father by clasping his hand, the hand-holding by the Judge,
Laurel, and Becky while the latter sinks toward death, Fay's
idle hands, clock hands, Phil's imaginary handshake with the
kamikaze pilot--all function expertly within this pattern. Even
the name of the town itself--Mt. Salus--suggests a welcome
greeting, as does Becky's name, and the last thing Laurel
sees as she leaves Mt. Salus are the hands of Adele Courtland's schoolchildren, "the many and unknown hands, wishing
her goodbye."

To identify themes and image patterns in this way does not, of course, account for the novel's dramatic power and formal excellence. But in addition to providing clues to the novel's meaning, it also helps to place The Optimist's Daughter within the Welty canon. For though the novel may appear to be the most "realistic" (i. e. , close to literal) of her major works, it is in fact a kind of lyric meditation on the themes that have always concerned her. The patterns of her art may be more transparent here, but certainly not simpler. The Optimist's Daughter manifests that clarity of vision which is the mark of a great artist, and to borrow a phrase from Maritain, in apprehending the radiance of form in the novel we are really gazing at "the radiance of a mystery. "

I

Throughout the first two-thirds of The Optimist's Daughter we are given little or no interior view of Laurel McKelva Hand, for strategic reasons I have in part suggested. She is presented as a reacting observer to the events around her; rarely do we see her reflecting on experience, especially on present events in terms of the past. Like the unnamed heroine of Welty's early story, "A Memory," Laurel is both a focusing instrument for the action and subject for the author's treatment of the dual mysteries of the relationship between the public and private self and the relationship between memory and experience. "The mystery in how little we know of other people is no greater than the mystery of how much," Laurel reflects midway through the novel, and this mystery is at the heart of her own predicament. [1] A true child of her mother Becky, who "simply assumed her privacy," Laurel tries to assume it to the point of complete inviolability, so that the past, which she has patterned by memory, might remain frozen intact, like an interior dream. Until her final harrowing night in the house, Laurel moves through the novel in a numb somnambulistic state, locked in her private world. She is undeniably grief-stricken, and she submits rather helplessly to the grotesque public ceremony of the Judge's funeral. But Laurel's withdrawn, sensitive reaction to the mawkish display is due not only to her deep love for her parents; it bears upon her own character and especially her marriage to Phil Hand. Her attempt to save the memory of her father from violation is precisely what she has achieved in memorializing her brief marriage to Phil, evidenced by the fact that Laurel tends to withdraw even further whenever anyone mentions her marriage. Theirs was an idyllic union, a "dream"

of happiness, now locked in Laurel's memory, an idealized
pattern no longer subject to the disruptive, yet vitalizing
forces of life. But the price she is forced to pay is the
terrible recognition later that what she and Phil missed was
life itself, the joy and agony of human contact, the "protecting" and "protesting," which indelibly shapes a relationship.
Laurel may indeed have had her ideal marriage (that her
attendants are still referred to as "The Bridesmaids" further
suggests its unfulfillment), but it was not the life of anguish
and love which, having been lived, would not demand private
memorialization. In Welty's fiction, as Robert Penn Warren
has noted, the dream must always be submitted to the fact,
to the flux of life with all its terrors and violations. And
this is why, certainly, Laurel must face and "have it out"
with Fay Chisom at the end of the novel: it is a mark of
her reawakening and growth in self-knowledge, a victory over
that part of herself which would preserve her from the raw
shocks of life.

The corollary pattern to Laurel's situation, and the
obverse reflection of the private versus public self theme,
is represented by Fay Chisom and all other characters in
the novel who echo her behavior in kind--"the great, interrelated family of those who never know the meaning of what
has happened to them" (103). That is, they are incapable
of meaningful reflection and recollection, incapable of creating the vital pattern between memory and life. In addition
to Fay, there are the "blundering" Mardi Gras revelers who
form an appropriate backdrop for Judge McKelva's death;
Major Bullock, who "lived his life through others"; the Chisom clan, with the notable exception of Grandpa and Wendall;
and Mr. Cheek, the Mt. Salus jack-of-all-trades. Because
they assume no privacy, life for them is a matter of public
display; they can only blunder forward from moment to moment, unaware of any continuity to experience. Nevertheless,
in the very spontaneity of their blundering they represent an
effective counterfoil--an opposite extreme--to Laurel's spiritual numbness and detachment. And Welty gives them their
due, balancing the forces which tend toward an extreme ordering of life, frequently to the point of sterility, against the
chaotic but vital forces which inevitably disrupt the fixed pattern, a theme she has developed extensively throughout her
fiction, especially in The Golden Apples.

The death of Judge Clinton McKelva is, of course,
the central episode upon which vision and pattern focus in
the opening section of the novel. The New Orleans setting

is appropriate not only for the image of "blundering" revelry
it provides, and Fay's mindless attraction to it, but also as
a leitmotif for the Judge's own shallow optimism, which is
about to undergo its severest test. Though he is benignly
optimistic, his marriage to Fay has in fact, we learn, been
a betrayal of Becky and the past, and his eye disorder is
emblematic of the flaw in his optimistic vision. He informs
Dr. Courtland that the eye disturbance dates from Washington's
Birthday when, while pruning the rosebush called "Becky's
Climber," he began "seeing behind" himself. The fact that
he chose the wrong day to prune is significant, evidence as
he says that his "memory has slipped." Thus the flaw in
his seeing is linked to a flaw in his memory. Having betrayed the past in favor of the future, the Judge must now
face the consequences of his denial. As in the case of Laurel
later, memory is about to come due for the Judge, claiming
its right by disrupting the pattern of optimism he has created,
a shock which Laurel perceives in the changed expression on
her father's face. Outside on the street after his eye examination, she wonders "what he was seeing," and concludes
that he appears "for the first time in her memory a man ad-
mitting to a little uncertainty in his bearings."

Welty does not reveal the meaning of the incident at
Becky's Climber which precipitated the Judge's illness until
after his funeral, another example of her strategic structur-
ing of events to redouble the thematic effect of memory's
relationship to experience. We learn first that "Judge Mc-
Kelva had recalled himself at Becky's Climber" [my italics].
And what he recalled, specifically, was an earlier scene with
Becky pruning and the Judge looking on. On that occasion,
Becky wondered aloud about the history of the rosebush ("That
old root there may be a hundred years old!"), while the
Judge, giving her his "saturnine smile," answers: "Strong
as an old apple tree!" The scene is one of apparent bliss
in their marriage before Becky's illness, but beneath this
surface lies the root of Judge McKelva's betrayal, for his
saturnine smile and ready answer are in fact a form of doting on Becky, the same doting he later applies to Fay. Now,
in the extremity of his present eye ailment, it is the betrayal implicit in his own vision that the Judge must face:
memory has resurrected it.

Does Judge McKelva, after his operation, come to
terms with his betrayal, his shallow optimism? Welty
shrouds his final days in mystery so that we get no interior
view, though to Laurel he seems to be "paying some unbar-

gained for price for his recovery. " "Recalling himself" in the scene at Becky's Climber may have triggered a series of revelations which force the Judge to see that his optimism has been an indulgent evasion of the tragic, especially since he <u>became</u> an optimist (he really always was one) precisely at that point in Becky's decline when he could no longer face her dying without concocting the lie that he would take her back to West Virginia. His lie was another example of doting, and doting, as Becky knew ("Lucifer! Liar!"), was a denial of her very person, just as "unliving" as his patronizing of Fay. Like his daughter Laurel, Judge McKelva had given up the "protesting" for the "protecting" in a human relationship. He may "see" the betrayal implicit in this in his final days; Welty suggests that his vision may be undergoing a radical evaluation. He lies almost lifeless, without hope in spite of Laurel's attempts to reach him by talk and reading. Later, she tells Fay that her father was "concentrating on his life," but whatever illumination he might be achieving is left, pathetically, unshared. He lies with the window blinds closed against the danger of light, in a "dream of patience," never once expressing hope, a passive sufferer without any "protesting" for life and love, as Becky did. And when the Judge dies, Dr. Courtland's remark--"The renegade! I believe he just plain sneaked out on us!"--is a fitting pronouncement on his whole life, suggesting that in death, as in his doting, the Judge escaped from the protracted agony of suffering, humiliation and defeat which Becky underwent in her five-year decline into death.[2] Between Judge McKelva and his daughter there is no final scene of desolation and "love's deep anger"; there is instead only the failure of speech, and the Judge's limp hand which tries to communicate some final private mystery that Laurel cannot quite fathom.

The state of Laurel's own interior vision is also shrouded in the opening section of the novel, and the quality of remoteness and ordered detachment which typifies her approach to life is for that very reason quite evident. Like her mother, Laurel is an orderer: She is repulsed by the Mardi Gras revelers, and after her father's operation she at once establishes a patterned schedule of sitting with him every day. How strongly this trait marks her character is apparent even on the chaotic night of her father's death, when, as she rushes down the hospital corridor to the dying Judge, Laurel reflects that she had "never noticed the design in the tiling before, like some clue she would need to follow to get to the right place." But like her father, Laurel is also about to receive a shocking blow to her patterned vision of experience,

forcing involvement and self-examination. As the Judge falters, she is immersed in chaos and disorder--"blundering"--
and Welty represents the movement by a pattern of images
centered on water and immersion, suggesting the necessary
rite of passage and symbolic death Laurel is about to undergo.

As we might expect, Welty's focus is on what Laurel
does, and doesn't, see. When she first enters her father's
room after the operation, it is "like a no where. At first,
she did not realize that she could see the bridge--it stood
out there dull in the distance, its function hardly evident,
as if it were only another building. The river was not visible. She lowered the blind against the wide white sky that
reflected it. "3 Here, Laurel is not on the bridge, patterning
the vision she receives, as in the crucial bridge scene with
Phil. Rather, she is immersed in something disruptive,
suggestive of the breakdown of order which culminates a few
weeks later in Fay's assault on the Judge. And on that occasion, when Laurel rushes into his room she first sees "a
watery constellation ... throbbing and near. She was looking
straight out at the whole Mississippi River Bridge in lights. "
Against Dr. Courtland's orders, Fay has opened the window
blind, and now Laurel is too late to save her father. "His
whole pillowless head went dusky, as if he laid it under the
surface of dark, pouring water and held it there. " There is
no detached perspective or vision for Laurel here; she is
literally flooded with chaos and grief as her father's life
sinks from her grasp. Thus Laurel's new condition is conveyed imagistically as she journeys on the train from New
Orleans with the body of her father. "Set deep in the swamp,
where the black trees were welling with buds like red drops,
was one low beech that had kept its last year's leaves, and
it appeared to Laurel to travel along with their train, gliding
at a magic speed through the cypresses they left behind. It
was her own reflection in the windowpane--the beach tree was
her head. Now it was gone. As the train left the black
swamp and pulled out into the space of Pontchartrain, the
window filled with a featureless sky over pale smooth water,
where a seagull was hanging with wings fixed, like a stopped
clock on a wall. "4 Here there is no bridge, and instead of
the confluence of the rivers there is only the stagnant black
swamp, and Laurel is "headless," immersed in a flow of
disruptive forces both external and internal. Pattern and
vision are overwhelmed here, though they will reemerge to
claim their value for Laurel in the end.

II

Pattern and vision, interwoven by theme and imagery, are extended and deepened throughout the second section of the novel, centered on Judge McKelva's funeral. Again, Welty controls the developing vision through the subtle use of image patterns--fire, water, birds, feeding, touching, and designing itself. Emphasis here is on the public ceremony, but Welty uses the funeral skillfully to penetrate the mystery of human relationships, focusing on Laurel's own predicament. For Laurel the whole public display of the funeral is a grotesque violation of her father's life, perpetrated by the vulgar Fay and her family, and also by her Mt. Salus neighbors, whose memories of the Judge seem quite distorted. But Laurel herself is not immune from this failing, as we shall see later. She judges the failings of the mourners severely, as indeed Becky would have, and one of the ironies of the novel is that it is mother and daughter who have judgmental vision, not the doting Clinton McKelva. Though we may fault the Judge's doting optimism, it is also important to see Welty's criticism of the judgmental vision of Becky and the Laurel of the early sections of the novel. Judging in its severest form represents an attempt to narrow and fix reality, a reduction of mystery which can be as life-denying as doting. In short, doting and judging are opposite extremes of vision, both distortive insofar as they attempt to impose a fixed pattern on the fluid mystery of reality. Laurel eventually comes to see this, and thus "stand between" her parents' different world views, but not before the failings of both views are revealed in the mourners and in herself.

Under the double shock of her father's death and Fay's vulgarity, Laurel initially seeks refuge in the idyllic order provided by memory, as yet unassailable before the funeral begins. Her first night in Mt. Salus she retires to her room and, just before sleep, recalls a beautiful memory from childhood of her parents reading. "In the lateness of the night, their two voices reading to each other where she could hear them, never letting a silence divide or interrupt them, combined into one unceasing voice and wrapped her around as she listened, as still as if she were asleep. She was sent to sleep under a velvety cloak of words, richly patterned and stitched with gold, straight out of a fairy tale, while they went reading on into her dreams."[5] It is an ideal scene between Becky and the Judge, one that Laurel would like to preserve intact, as perhaps she would like to preserve herself in an invulnerable state, but such a vision must be submitted to the new events about to unfold at the Judge's funeral, and Laurel must readjust that memory to new perceptions.

Thus the whole series of events surrounding Judge McKelva's funeral constitute a shocking, but vitalizing, assault on Laurel's protected sensibility. In addition to Fay's desecration of the house, Laurel must also contend with the Mt. Salus mourners, who persistently evoke inaccurate memories of the Judge. One of the worst offenders is Major Bullock, an example in extremis of the Judge's optimism. Bullock continually dotes on Fay, ignoring her selfishness; he drinks throughout the funeral to blunt the harsh fact of death, and it is he who summons the disruptive Chisom clan, though the Judge requested it before dying. The latter group --with the exception of Grandpa Chisom and Wendall--not only embody more of the blundering forces Laurel must contend with; they also, like the Dalzells, represent variations on the major theme of the wanderer and the attachment to home. This theme is dominant in Delta Wedding, The Golden Apples, and Losing Battles: the family as both vital center and/or threatening enclosure which stifles the self. Conversely, Welty frequently examines the predicament of the wanderers, those who leave home to assert a selfhood, who may succeed in finding it or may become "lost," disaffected and rootless loners. [6] The Chisom clan, as Fay's mother insists, believe in "clustering just as close as we can get," and the image of a stifling communality, one in which the private self is virtually denied, is manifested in their bumptious behavior-- public displays such as Fay's "scenes"--throughout the funeral. Welty echoes the pattern deeper and deeper, as Chisom family experience reflects the earlier blunderers, the Dalzells. Like Grandpa Dalzell, Mr. Chisom died of cancer and could only take "tap water," and both families have disaffected, wanderer sons. Archie Lee, Mr. Dalzell's "long lost" son, retreats into drink as his father is dying, refusing to see him because he's convinced, wrongly, that "he don't know I'm living." Roscoe Chisom wandered from the Chisom clan to Orange, Texas and committed suicide. Characteristically, Mrs. Chisom cannot understand what was "fretting" her son; she only learns that "Roscoe didn't want me to know." Whatever drove Roscoe Chisom to suicide, he insisted to the end on complete disaffection from his family. The paradox of the private versus the communal self, the wanderer-family tie theme, is of course also exhibited in the McKelva family, all of whom left home to marry and find a new life, but Welty's extension of the pattern to include the Chisoms and Dalzells is but another instance of her almost flawless structuring of the novel.

While it is true that many of the recollections of
Judge McKelva by his Mt. Salus neighbors are inaccurate,
Welty nevertheless links him with a spirit of revelry which,
at its worst, may involve doting and an escape from harsh
reality, but at its best represents a vital, spontaneous joy
that is a rhythmic counterpoint to the dour seriousness--the
judging--of a Becky McKelva. The Judge's funeral has about
it the flavor of a social occasion, much to the chagrin of
Laurel; indeed, it is bizarre at times, replete with comic
figures and episodes. For example, Judge McKelva's former
secretary, Dot, recalls how he assuaged her guilty conscience
when she spent thirty-five dollars for a set of Mah-Jong. To
be sure the Judge's solicitude was another instance of doting,
but it also paid tribute to the spontaneous, self-fulfilling im-
pulses in the human spirit. The same ambiguity is evident
in the story about the family cook, Missouri. She was wounded
witnessing a gunfight, and the Judge brought her home and
"kept her safe under his own roof." Again, he protected,
whereas Becky might simply have judged Missouri or approved
Dot's self-recrimination, and yet his impulse did convert potential tragedy into good, just as his optimism about the terrible flood did finally issue in an oil discovery that brought
financial security and helped Dr. Courtland through medical
school.

As in most of her works, Welty uses music as emblem of the joyous spirit and creative self-assertion, and
here this spirit is specifically linked with Judge McKelva.
Verna Longmier, the "crazy" Mt. Salus sewing woman, recalls how she and the Judge would lead out the Christmas
dance each year in the McKelva home. Later, we learn of
the great pains to which the Judge went to hire an orchestra
from New Orleans for Laurel's wedding, celebrated at the
country club with the "best" dance floor, a club which subsequently burned down, like Becky's home in West Virginia.
And old Tom Farris, the blind piano tuner, makes his appearance at the Judge's funeral, as does the entire Mt. Salus
High School band, whose new uniforms the Judge had pur-
chased. Through these recollections, Welty forces us to ap-
praise the Judge with a wider sympathy than Becky's severe
last view of her husband.

For her part, Laurel is increasingly horrified at the
public spectacle of her father's funeral and .she battles gal-
lantly to protect his sacred memory. But though the memories of the Judge's friends are largely distorted, for Welty
this is an inevitable fact in the rivalry between memory and

experience, one to be accepted rather than challenged. Laurel's
sense of grief and outrage is understandable, but Welty is
quick to show the narrowness in her heroine's attempt to preserve a frozen memory of her parents, and that the breaking
of Laurel's private shell of inviolability is necessary to ex-
pand her vision. Laurel finds it impossible to "protect" her
deceased father throughout the funeral; her own plans, geared
to insure privacy, are upset at every turn. Her anger reaches
a climax when Major Bullock insists that the Judge faced down
a mob of Klan-like "White Caps." "'He's trying to make my
father into something he wanted to be himself,' Laurel insists.
'They're misrepresenting him--falsifying, that's what Mother
would call it. '"[7]

Like Becky, Laurel judges, but Welty submits her
judgment to the broader vision of Adele Courtland, the novel's
chief voice of wisdom. When Laurel insists that the Judge
would never stand for lies being told about him, Adele replies: "Yes he would.... If the truth might hurt the wrong
person." Nevertheless, Laurel insists self-righteously: "I'm
his daughter. I want what people say now to be the truth."
But this moralistic stance is immediately undercut by Laurel's
sudden recognition of her own failure of memory. "She had
not read her father the book he'd wanted after all. The wrong
book! The wrong book! She was looking at her own mistake,
and its long shadow reaching back to join the others."[8] So
Laurel too is complicit, and her failure to read her sick father
the right book contrasts sharply with the idyllic memory of
her parents reading, their voices patterned in harmony, from
the night before. Now, all she can say feebly is: "The
least anybody can do for him is remember right," and the
remark is an admission of her own vulnerability, the weakness of a vision that attempts to fix memory into a pattern
divorced from life. And with Fay's violent outburst at the
bier, Laurel's vain attempt to protect her father is irrevocably destroyed. "Mr. Pitts had achieved one illusion, that
danger to his lived life was still alive; now there was no
longer that."

III

After the funeral of her father, Laurel still remains
frozen within her private world, where memory and pattern
serve her as defenses against "blundering" reality. To her
grief has been added Fay's outrageous behavior during the
funeral, and Laurel, unforgiving, condemns Fay and wishes

to exact recognition from her of her sins. Laurel's vision
here is, of course, narrowly self-righteous and vindictive,
a fact which she must come to recognize herself. But before exploring Laurel's state of mind, Welty again uses Adele
Courtland as a means of putting the events of the funeral in
true perspective. While cardinals and mockingbirds sing and
sport in the trees overhead, Laurel's friends sit in the yard
and discuss the Judge, Fay, and the funeral. Unlike the
other self-righteous witnesses, Adele defends Fay to the extent of pointing out that, within her own limitations, her behavior was no more of a failing than the Judge's Mt. Salus
neighbors'. Like Becky, Adele is an admitted pessimist in
her estimation of human character, but unlike both Becky
and Laurel, Adele recognizes compassionately that mere judgment of human behavior is rarely equal to its fluid mystery;
it is, in fact, a form of blindness to that mystery. Consequently, Adele addresses her defense of Fay specifically to
Laurel, pointing out that Fay was simply emulating her mother.
"We can't find fault with that, can we, Laurel?'" Adele asks.
Finding fault, of course, is what Becky would have done, and
ironically, it is precisely what Laurel is doing now, emulating her mother. Yet she refuses to pity Fay, and responds
to Adele: "I hope I never see her again. "

Laurel's vindictive attitude and closed heart reveal
the persistence of her desire to preserve an idealized memory of her parents and an inviolately private self. Thus she
objects vehemently to her friends' story-telling about the
Judge and Becky, accusing them of "laughing at" her parents.
Later, she examines the family library, her father's books
and papers, but finds no letters from her father to her mother. And how fitting, given the pattern of "hands" and "work"
in the novel, that Laurel does find traces of Fay in the fin-
gernail polish stains on the Judge's desk, which she immediately erases as completely as she would like to obliterate
both the person and the memory of her antagonist. Nevertheless, Laurel's protective instinct has become lifedenying,
a fact Welty keynotes at this point by introducing Laurel's
first recollection of her marriage to Phil Hand. Viewing
their wedding picture on her father's desk, she recalls that
he had given it "a silver frame," and this memory sparks
an insight into her marriage: "So had she. Her marriage
had been of magical ease, of ease--of brevity and conclusion
and all belonging to Chicago and not here. " Of course the
fact that it is a silver-framed photograph--photo and memory
"framing" the experience into a pattern as the girl in "A
Memory" frames experience with her hands--puts that life

at one remove from vivifying reality. Nevertheless, with
this crucial first interior view of Laurel, Welty begins to
open her heroine to explicit self-reflection and a dynamic
encounter with memory.

Laurel's night journey begins with the intrusion of the
chimney swift, a "blundering, frantic" bird she at once associates with all the blundering forces of life and particularly
with Fay's assault on her dying father, so that like the nurse
she wants to cry out: "Abuse! Abuse!" Characteristically,
Laurel first tries to fit the experience into a pattern. "Try
to put it in the form of facts, she ordered herself. For the
person who wishes to do so, it is possible to assail a helpless man; it is only necessary to be married to him. It is
possible to say to the dying 'Enough is enough,' if the listener
who overhears is his daughter with his memory to protect.
The facts were a verdict, and Laurel lived with this verdict
in her head, walking up and down. "⁹ Laurel wants Fay to
acknowledge her sins--"This would be a fact"--but to reduce
the mystery to a set of facts to be judged is a deadening
vision which condemns the accuser as well as the accused.
Laurel's grim desire for satisfaction is the extreme form of
her mother's judgmental vision, yet, to her credit, Laurel
has an intimation of the danger of this position. "Have I
come to be as lost a soul as the soul Fay exposed to Father,
and to me? Because unlike Father, I cannot feel pity for
Fay." Yet neither can Laurel relinquish self-righteousness;
she "can't stop realizing it.... Why, it would stand up in
court!... Fay betrayed herself: I'm released, she thought
...." (The legal language used here is, of course, highly
significant.) But Laurel is not released; like the bird, she
is trapped, blundering within this perspective, this pattern
of vision. She wants to present "the damnable evidence" to
her mother, and so find consolation, but in contemplating
this longing she discovers "the horror" of her stance. "Father, beginning to lose his sight, followed Mother, but who am
I at the point of following but Fay? Laurel thought. The
scene she had just imagined, herself confiding the abuse to
her mother, and confiding it in all tenderness, was a more
devastating one than all Fay had acted out in the hospital.
What would I not do, perpetrate, she wondered, for consolation?"¹⁰

The frantic blundering of the chimney swift drives
Laurel into the sewing room, where she slept in infancy and
where now fresh memories of her childhood and of her parents' life and death begin to thaw her spiritual numbness.

Structurally, the entire section is brilliantly patterned by
Welty, with technique redoubling theme as memory is brought
vividly to life to vitalize and widen Laurel's vision. Laurel
initially recalls the "firelight and warmth" of the now cold
sewing room, and this evokes the idyllic memory of when
she "sat on this floor and put together the fallen scraps of
cloth into stars, flowers, birds, people, or whatever she
liked to call them, lining them up, spacing them out, making
them into patterns, families, on the sweet-smelling matting,
with the shine of firelight, or the summer light, moving over
mother and child and what they both were making."11 But
the idyll gives way to deeper recollections, memories of her
yearly visits to her mother's home in West Virginia, and the
central memory of her fear of feeding pegeons, Welty's complex symbol for Laurel's fear of life "up close" and the whole
mystery of human relationships--violation and sustenance,
protecting and protesting, love and separateness. She remembers watching "a pair of them sticking their beaks down
each other's throats, gagging each other, eating out of each
other's craws," and they "convinced her that they could not
escape each other and could not themselves be escaped from."
Though Laurel still fears birds "up close," what the memory
of the pigeons now gives her is an insight into her mother's
youthful innocence, and more importantly, a perception of the
limits of Becky's judgmental vision. "No more than Laurel
had known that rivers ran clear and sang over rocks might
her mother have known that her mother's pigeons were waiting to pluck each other's tongues out. 'Up home,' just as
Laurel was in Mt. Salus, her mother was too happy to know
what went on in the outside world. Besides, when her mother looked closely, it was not in order to see pigeons but to
verify something--the truth or a mistake; hers or anothers."12
[My italics.] But Laurel also recalls her mother's courage
and fidelity to her dying father in the river journey to Baltimore, and this memory illuminates the depths of her own
despair of life. "Neither of us saved our fathers, Laurel
thought. But Becky was the brave one. I stood in the hall
too, but I did not any longer believe that anyone could be
saved, anyone at all. Not from others."13

　　　Laurel's judgment of herself is excessively severe;
it is the kind of judgment Becky might have made against
herself. Laurel's journey to self-knowledge will take her
"beyond" this vision, and free her from it, but not before
she has given the past its full due. Now the memory of her
mother's last years resurrects itself, revealing both the
strength and tragic failure of her parents' relationship, of

both their ways of seeing, and revealing also the pathetic incompleteness of Laurel's own life. At the onset of her mother's illness, when Becky's vision began to falter, Laurel critically judged both her father's helplessness and her mother's deepening pessimism. Naively, she believed the powers which create pattern--memory and self-perception--would be an adequate defense against the blundering force of illness: "Her mother had only to recollect herself!" Becky does try to defend herself with memory--reciting rhymes from her childhood McGuffey's Reader--but memory fails in the end, so that she cannot even recognize the Judge and Laurel. And recalling this now, Laurel sees both the inadequacy and the self-serving nature of her rigorous attempts to pattern experience. "What burdens we lay on the dying, Laurel thought, as she listened now to the accelerated rain on the roof: seeking to prove some little thing that we can keep to comfort us when they can no longer feel--something incapable of being kept as of being proved: the lastingness of memory, vigilance against harm, self-reliance, good hope, trust in one another. "14

Recalling her mother's death teaches Laurel about the whole mysterious character of human relationships, but especially about the incompleteness of her own life. Dying, Becky is true to her judgmental vision in accusing Judge McKelva of being a "coward," but her anguish and accusation, as Laurel sees, is the measure of the depth of her love--"And still she held fast to their hands, to Laurel's too." Becky's accusation is a harsh indictment of the condescending denial of personhood implicit in the Judge's optimism. "He loved his wife. Whatever she did that she couldn't help doing was all right. Whatever she was driven to say was all right. But it was not all right! Her trouble was that very desperation. And no one had the power to cause that except the one she desperately loved, who refused to consider that she was desperate. It was betrayal on betrayal. "15 But Becky's fierce judgment also extends to her daughter; just before her death she condemns Laurel's distant, observer stance and her helplessness. "You could have saved your mother's life. But you stood by and wouldn't intervene. I despair of you."

And yet Becky's final judgment protests too much. How could Laurel have intervened and "saved" her? The answer can only be: No more than Becky was able to save her own father, or Laurel hers. Becky demands too much, more than is humanly possible. She may be heroic, but her severe vision of experience is as one-sided as the Judge's facile optimism, which Laurel now perceives in the mysterious "rivalry" in human relationships. "It's not between the living and the dead, between the old and the new; it's between too much love and too little. There is no rivalry as bitter; Laurel had seen its work."16 Laurel now understands how her father, for all his failings, suffered and died "worn out with both wives," and she is able to extend to both parents the vision of charity they deserve and which Welty claims for them.

With her own heart now opening, Laurel wishes she could bring her parents back to "any torment of living because that torment was something they had known together," and she recalls "her mother holding and holding onto their hands, her own and her father's holding onto her mother's, long after there was nothing more to be said." She understands now, painfully, that for all its betrayal and anguish, her parents did live a life with "love's deep anger," precisely what Laurel herself has missed, not only because of her husband Phil's death, but because of her fear of life itself. What "might have been" is brought home to her with crushing force in a remark of her Grandmother's she discovers in a letter: "I will try to send Laurel a cup of sugar for her birthday. Though if I can find a way to do it, I would like to send her one of my pigeons. It would eat from her hand if she would let it." The final sentence, of course, suggests how Laurel might conquer her fear of life through love, and as a "flood of feeling" descends on her now, her night journey culminates appropriately with the "resurrection" of Phil Hand and their incomplete life.

> If Phil could have lived--
> But Phil was lost. Nothing of their life together remained except in her own memory; love was sealed away in its perfection and had remained there.
> If Phil had lived--
> She had gone on with the old perfection undisturbed and undisturbing. Now, by her own hands, the past had been raised up, and he looked at her, Phil himself--here waiting, all the time, Lazarus. He looked at her out of eyes wild with the craving for his unlived life, with mouth open like a funnel's.17

Phil's longing for his unlived life, their unlived life, is pictured specifically in images of sustenance and feeding, echo-

ing the passage of the feeding pigeons from Laurel's childhood. Facing Phil's ghost, Laurel melts into tears "for what
happened to life," and as she grieves, Phil's demand echoes
with a roar throughout the house; "I wanted it! I wanted it!"

IV

After her painful night journey into the past, Laurel
awakens refreshed from a dream, a dream of the actual train
trip south she and Phil took just before their marriage. The
dream is one of joyous hope, their happiness at starting a
life together. During the night, memories of grief and loss
both shocked and revivified Laurel into a deeper vision of
her life; now memory serves to restore the idyllic pattern.
Significantly, Welty presents the vision through a commingling
of major image patterns. For what Laurel recalls especially
is the epiphanic moment when together she and Phil passed
above "the confluence of the waters" of the Ohio and Mississippi, watching a line of birds in the distance against the sky-
line. The vision is carefully patterned and "perfect," with
everything in its ordered place. "All they could see was
sky, water, birds, light, and confluence. It was the whole
morning world." Laurel and Phil saw themselves as part
of this confluence, united together in faith and love, believing
that "we're going to live forever." And recalling this now,
Laurel realizes that the brief, idyllic period of their love is
indestructible. Memory is redemptive here, restoring an
order that transcends all the blundering forces of life. "Left
bodiless and graveless of a death made of water and fire in
a year long ago, Phil could still tell her of her life. For
her life, any life, was nothing but the continuity of its love."[18]

The memory of the train journey evokes more memories of Laurel's marriage of Phil, a marriage in which
"there had not been a single blunder...." It was Phil, as
his name suggests, who taught Laurel to love and to overcome
her own tendency to see love as protection. "Until she knew
Phil, she thought of love as shelter; her arms went out as
a naive offer of safety. He had showed her that this need
not be so. Protection, like self-protection, fell away from
her like all one garment, some anachronism foolishly saved
from childhood."[19] With equal care Phil taught her how to
use her hands, how "to work toward and into her pattern,
not to sketch peripheries." Himself a designer of houses,
Phil is a perfectionist in all that he makes, but he is realist
enough to know that pattern and "perfection" are fragile hu-

man creations that of themselves do not guarantee the vital
life nor protect against its blundering forces. Laurel sees
now that he "was not an optimist ... Phil had learned everything he could manage to learn, and done as much as he had
time for, to design houses to stand, to last, to be lived in;
but he had known they could equally well, with the same de-
votion and timeless effort, be built of cards."[20] Thus when
war breaks out, Phil chooses to serve on a minesweeper
rather than work in "camouflage," and when Judge McKelva
asked how close he has come to kamikaze pilots, Phil replies: "About close enough to shake hands with...."

Before achieving her final vision, Laurel must still
contend with "blundering" forces, but her very capacity and
willingness to do this now is the measure of her growth.
First she and the cook Missouri are able to release the frantic chimney swift from the house; then Laurel is able to fend
successfully against that blundering violator of privacy, Mr.
Cheek. But it is her final, unexpected encounter with Fay
Chisom which produces Laurel's greatest epiphany, one that
illuminates the mysterious truth upon which the novel, both
thematically and structurally, is based.

Fay's unexpected reappearance brings Laurel, who
still believes she must defend the past from violation, to the
dangerous point of becoming a severe vindicator and judge.
She accuses Fay of desecrating the house and all the love
and loyalty from the past it embodies, and her accusation
leads her to answer a question she could not answer earlier:
Why her father married Fay? Now Laurel sees the pattern
behind the relationship.

> Experience did, finally, get set into its
> right order, which is not always the order of other
> people's time. Her mother had suffered in life
> every symptom of having been betrayed, and it was
> not until she had died, and the protests of memory
> came due, that Fay had ever tripped in from Ma-
> drid, Texas. It was not until that later moment,
> perhaps, that her father himself had ever dreamed
> of a Fay. For Fay was Becky's own dread. What
> Becky had felt, and had been afraid of, might have
> existed here in the house all the time, for her.
> Past and future might have changed places, in some
> convulsion of the mind, but that could do nothing to
> impugn the truth of the heart. Fay could have
> walked in early as well as late, she could have
> come at anytime at all. She was coming.[21]

Still, the sight of Becky's damaged breadboard, and
Fay's utter insensitivity to its value as symbol of "the whole
solid past," almost drives Laurel into the blunder of trying
to exact retribution; ironically, an act of violence that would
be similar to Fay's abuse of the Judge for ignoring her "needs."
Laurel holds the breadboard above her head, and "for a moment it seemed to be what supported her, a raft in the water,
to keep her from slipping down deep, where the others had
gone before her." The image echoes here, linking the scene
with Phil's and the Judge's deaths, and indicating the "death"
Laurel may undergo if all she can see her way clear to do
is to punish Fay. But what saves her from striking Fay is
the memory of Wendall, the "unfalsifying, unvindictive" Chisom whom Laurel wanted to protect at the funeral. Here,
the memory of human vulnerability and sensitivity restrains
Laurel, and her restraint acts as a grace which frees her
from her desire to vindicate the past and brings her her
culminating vision.

> "I know you aren't anything to the past,"
> she said. "You can't do anything to it now." And
> neither am I; and neither can I, she thought, al-
> though it has been everything and done everything
> to me, everything for me. The past is no more
> open to help or hurt than was Father in his coffin.
> The past is like him, impervious, and can never
> be awakened. It is memory that is the somnam-
> bulist. It will come back in its wounds across the
> world, like Phil, calling us by our names and de-
> manding its rightful tears. It will never be im-
> pervious. The memory can be hurt, time and
> again--but in that may lie its final mercy. As
> long as it's vulnerable to the living moment, it
> lives for us, and while it lives, and while we are
> able, we can give it up its due....
> Memory lived not in the initial possession
> but in the freed hands, pardoned and freed, and
> in the heart that can empty and fill again, in the
> patterns restored by dreams. [22]

Relinquishing the breadboard, Laurel herself is freed,
and as she hurries away from Mt. Salus, carrying with her
her new vision of life's mercy, she receives one final gesture of loving "freed" hands: Adele Courtland's schoolchildren waving to her, "the twinking of their hands, the many
small and unknown hands, wishing her goodbye."

Notes

[1] Eudora Welty, The Optimist's Daughter (New York: Random House, 1972), p. 81. All further references are to this edition.

[2] The same point is made elsewhere in Mrs. Chisom's remark at the Judge's bier that he looks hardly "wasted," and in Laurel's remark to Adele that her father's illness "wasn't like Mother's." Also, there are several phrases used in reference to the Judge--e.g. "playing possum," "sneaking out," "rambling"--which suggest a pattern of evasion. In one sense his death might be seen as an escape from painful revelation, symbolically concentrated in and epitomized by Fay's assault on him.

[3] The Optimist's Daughter, p. 14.

[4] Ibid., p. 45.   [5] Ibid., p. 57-8.

[6] Fay's lie to Laurel, in which she repudiates her family, is an obvious manifestation of this pattern.

[7] The Optimist's Daughter, p. 83.

[8] Ibid., p. 83.   [9] Ibid., pp. 130-31.

[10] Ibid., p. 132.   [11] Ibid., pp. 133-34.

[12] Ibid., p. 141.   [13] Ibid., p. 144.

[14] Ibid., p. 146.   [15] Ibid., p. 150.

[16] Ibid., p. 152.   [17] Ibid., p. 154.

[18] Ibid., p. 160.   [19] Ibid., p. 161.

[20] Ibid., p. 162.   [21] Ibid., p. 174.

[22] Ibid., p. 179.

NOTES ON CONTRIBUTORS

John Alexander Allen's poems have appeared in many periodicals and anthologies, and collected in The Hollins Poets (1965) and The Lean Divider (1968). His essays "Bottom and Titania" and "Dogberry" appeared in Shakespeare Quarterly and will be included in his forthcoming book, Shakespeare's Comic Heroes. His essay "Eudora Welty: The Three Moments" was first delivered in her presence at the Hollins College Celebration for Eudora Welty. Mr. Allen is professor of English at Hollins College.

M. E. Bradford, associate professor of English at the University of Dallas, has published 150 essays on British and American literature. His recent work includes Rumors of Mortality: An Introduction to Allen Tate (1969); the collection he edited, The Form Discovered: Essays on the Achievement of Andrew Lytle (1973); and the forthcoming Of Pride and Humility: Studies in Faulkner's Short Fiction.

Charles E. Davis has published numerous essays on Southern literature, among them "The South in Eudora Welty's Fiction: A Changing World," in Studies in American Fiction; "The Wilderness Delivered: Irony in James Dickey's Deliverance"; and "William Faulkner's Joe Christmas: A Rage for Order," in Arizona Quarterly. Mr. Davis teaches at the University of North Carolina-Greensboro.

John F. Desmond has published several articles on Flannery O'Connor in the Southern Humanities Review, Mississippi Quarterly, Flannery O'Connor Bulletin, and other journals. He has also published essays on Faulkner, Bernard Malamud, and Graham Greene, and his short stories have appeared in the Michigan Quarterly Review, Descant, and the Texas Quarterly. Mr. Desmond teaches at Whitman College.

Barbara Fialkowski is an assistant professor of English and creative writing at Bowling Green State University

139

in Ohio. She has published essays on Parker Tyler and
Frank O'Hara, and has published poetry in Shenandoah, New
Letters, Poetry Now, and many other literary journals.

Albert J. Griffith is professor of English and vice
president and dean of academic affairs at Our Lady of the
Lake University in San Antonio. He is the author of a critical study of Peter Taylor (Twayne, 1971) and has published
critical articles on numerous Southern writers in Modern
Fiction Studies, Shenandoah, Studies in Short Fiction, Georgia
Review and many other journals.

Jerry Harris is chairman of the Division of Humanities at Pikeville College in Kentucky. He has recently
written a book-length study of the short stories of Eudora
Welty.

William McMillen has published essays on Eudora
Welty, Allen Tate, and Vance Bourjaily. His short stories
have appeared in Prairie Schooner and North American Review. Mr. McMillen teaches at Bowling Green State University in Ohio.

Douglas Messerli, who teaches at the University of
Maryland, has published Djuna Barnes: A Bibliography and,
with Howard N. Fox, The Index to Periodical Fiction. He
has also written articles on Faulkner, Hart, Crane, Eudora
Welty, John Weiners, Frank O'Hara, Wyndham Lewis and
Ezra Pound. Mr. Messerli is editor of Sun & Moon: A
Quarterly of Literature and Là-bas: a newsletter of exper-
imental poetry and poetics.

D. James Neault is the author of several essays on
Ezra Pound, including "Appolonius of Tyana: The Odyssean
Hero of Rock Drill as a Doer of Holiness" and "Richard of
St. Victor and Rock Drill," both published in Paedeuma. He
is also a Latin contributor to The Companion: An Annotated
Index of the Cantos of Ezra Pound. Currently Mr. Neault
is working on book-length studies of the Cantos of Pound and
the drama of Denis Johnston.

INDEX

141